1001 Bible Questions Kids Ask

1001 Bible Questions Kids Ask

ZONDERVAN®

ZONDERVAN.com/
AUTHORTRACKER
follow your favorite authors

We want to hear from you. Please send your comments about this book to us in care of zreview@zondervan.com. Thank you.

ZONDERVAN

1001 Bible Questions Kids Ask
Copyright © 2012 by Zonderkidz

This title is also available as a Zondervan ebook.
Visit www.zondervan.com/ebooks.

Requests for information should be addressed to:
Zonderkidz, 5300 Patterson Ave SE, Grand Rapids, Michigan 49530

ISBN: 978-0-310-72515-2

Compiled by Sarah Krueger
Cover designer: Mark Veldheer
Cover illustration: André Jolicoeur/Doodle Machine
Interior design: Ben Fetterley, Greg Johnson/Textbook Perfect

Printed in the United States of America

12 13 14 15 16 /DPM/ 19 18 17 16 15 14 13 12 11 10 9 8 7 6 5 4 3 2 1

Introduction

Have you ever been reading the Bible when you started wondering about things? Wondering about where the Garden of Eden is located (Question #5)? Or wondering how long a cubit really is (Question #989)? Or maybe even wondering why John the Baptist ate bugs while he was living in the desert (Question #722)? If you have been asking yourself questions like these, then this is the book for you.

1001 Bible Questions Kids Ask is a great resource for curious kid Bible readers. It actually does have 1,001 questions about things you will read about in the Bible. And it is so easy to use. Keep this book by your side whenever you are reading your Bible, and when you come to a word you need help with, or you don't recognize a Bible person's name, this book will be your perfect companion. Open up the book, find the book of the Bible you are reading by looking at the headings in the margin, and skim through the list of questions. You can even look for the specific verse reference following the question. Your question may be answered as easily as that!

1001 Bible Questions Kids Ask features:

- Questions that follow right along with the NIV Bible text

- Scripture reference following each question reflecting the verse that prompted each question

- A section of miscellaneous Bible questions that may help you answer some Bible mysteries

- An Index of Topics — in case you are searching for a certain subject

Old Testament

Genesis

1. Did God really create the universe?
(1) (Creation, God's Power)

Even though Christians have a wide range of opinions about the beginning of the universe, all can agree that God was the Creator. He created a perfect universe filled with stars and planets, and a perfect earth filled with an amazing variety of plants and animals.

2. Were the six days of creation actual 24-hour days? (1:5) (Creation, Time)

They could have been 24-hour days, or they could have been longer periods of time because the sun wasn't created until the fourth day.

3. Why did God rest on the seventh day? (2:2–3) (Creation, Sabbath)

He rested to set one day apart as holy because his creation work was finished.

4. What does the creation story teach us about our responsibility to the environment? (2) (Creation, Nature)

God first created Adam and "put him in the Garden of Eden to work it and take care of it" (Genesis 2:15). Christians should care for the environment not just for the sake of future generations, but as part of their obedient service to God.

5. Where was the Garden of Eden?
(2:8, 10–14) (Biblical Places)

Many people think Eden was probably in what is now the country of Iraq.

6. Why did God make the tree of the knowledge of good and evil?
(2:9) (Free Will, Sin)

God wanted his people to choose him freely. He gave humans the gift of free will; but unfortunately, they chose to disobey God.

7. Is it bad to know about good and evil? (2:17) (Sin)

☐➤ *Knowing evil* means experiencing it. God was testing their obedience. When they *experienced* evil, Adam and Eve brought sin and death into the world.

8. If God knew Adam and Eve were going to sin, why did he give them the choice to obey or not?

(3) (Free Will, Sin)

☐➤ God wanted his creatures and all of creation to be completely devoted to him and to serve him perfectly. In order for that to happen, Adam and Eve had to have the ability to choose; but unfortunately, they made the wrong decision.

9. If Eve was the one who talked to the serpent, isn't she responsible for the fall? (3:6) (Guilt, Sin)

It seems from verse six that Adam was with Eve. If he wasn't there, then he made the decision to disobey without the pressure from the serpent. He is just as guilty as she is.

10. Was it okay to marry two women? (4:19) (Ancient Practices, Marriage)

Having more than one wife was common in ancient times, but it goes against God's original plan for marriage.

11. How could people live such long lives? (5:5–32) (Age)

God's original plan was that people would live forever.

12. Why did God destroy other creatures besides humans with the flood? (6:7) (Animals, Sin)

☞ Human sin had contaminated everything God had made.

13. Is there a difference between a boat and an ark? (6:14) (Differences)

☞ An ark is much bigger than your average boat. The ark was about 450 feet long, 75 feet wide, and 45 feet high.

14. Did the flood cover the entire earth or was it more local? (7) (God's Power, Punishment)

☞ There are two opinions about the extent of the flood. The language in chapters 6 – 9 suggests that the flood was universal. Others think that a local, limited flood would have been enough to accomplish God's purpose of destroying all of the wicked people, while saving Noah and his family. In either case, the flood was a historical event that God used to punish the wicked and save those who believed in him.

15. Where are the mountains of Ararat? (8:4) (Biblical Places)

This mountain range was north of Mesopotamia and east of modern Turkey.

16. Why did Noah send out a dove?
(8:8–12) (God's Presence)

The raven he sent out first did not give him a clear answer. The dove eats only vegetation, so it could better tell Noah that land had reappeared.

17. Why is an olive leaf special?
(8:11) (Nature, Symbols)

Olive trees grow at lower elevations, and the fresh leaf told Noah that the water had receded enough for olive trees to grow again.

18. Why did God promise to never again destroy all living things?
(8:2–22) (Forgiveness, Promises)

God was pleased with Noah's sacrifice, showing forgiveness and grace for life on earth.

19. Why are there so many rules in the Bible about what we can and can't eat? (9:3) (Food, The Law)

While you're welcome to eat whatever you want to, God set out specific dietary rules in order to give us guidelines about what is healthy to eat.

20. Why is God's judgment on a murderer so severe? (9:5–6) (Judgment, Life, Murder, Sin)

God created human beings in his own image, so human life is sacred.

21. Why was the rainbow so important? (9:12–16) (Promises)

God wanted to remind people that his promise still stands and that he will never again destroy the world with a flood.

22. Why are these lists of names included in the Bible? (10:1–32) (Family, Names)

Genealogies record people's history and show how families were connected to the community. Many family trees in the Bible point forward and backward — forward to Jesus and backward to the people from whom he descended.

23. Why did God make people begin to speak different languages?
(11) (Languages)

God caused the people to speak different languages so they would be forced to separate themselves into different groups with different languages. This also meant that people would spread out into different parts of the earth, which was part of God's plan for the world.

24. Why did Abram let Lot choose his land first? (13:9, 14–17) (Promises)

☞ Abram remembered God's promise that all land would eventually come to Abram and his descendants. So Abram placed his confidence in God by giving Lot the first choice.

25. Why did God compare Abram's offspring to the dust of the earth?
(13:16) (Promises)

☞ God promised that the number of Abram's descendants would be so large that they would be hard to count.

26. Why is Abram called *the Hebrew?*
(14:13) (Names)

☞ Abram, the father of the Hebrew people, is the first person in the Bible to be called a Hebrew.

27. Why did Abram choose a servant to be his heir? **(15:2)** (Ancient Practices)

☞ In ancient times, a childless man could adopt a servant as his heir.

28. Why did God wait four generations before giving Abram's descendants the land? (15:16) (Waiting)

God wanted the Amorites, who lived in the land, to have plenty of time to repent of their sins.

29. Who was the angel of the Lord? (16:7) (Angels)

The angel was God's messenger, and some believe it was the human form in which God appeared to his people.

30. Why did God change Abram's name to Abraham? (17:5) (Ancient Practices, Names)

In ancient Hebrew culture, names signified a person's status and could be changed as one's status changed. Abraham means "father of many."

31. What is circumcision? (17:10) (Jewish Practices)

▭▶ Circumcision is a procedure in which the foreskin of the penis is removed, usually on the eighth day after birth. It was a sign of the covenant with God.

32. How did God appear to Abraham? (18:1) (God's Power, Talking to God)

▭▶ God appeared to Abraham in dreams or visions. Other times God spoke to him or took on a physical body.

33. Is anything too hard for God? (18:14) (God's Power)

▭▶ No. God is all-powerful, and he can accomplish his will even if it doesn't seem possible to us.

34. Does God forgive us when we fall back into an old habit? (20:2)

(Forgiveness, Sin)

Even people who have strong faith can experience times of weakness when they don't put all their trust in God. God will always forgive us if we ask, but he wants us to rely on him during hard times.

35. Why did Abraham lie about his wife again? (20:2) (Lying, Sin)

Abraham was trying to get out of a difficult situation on his own rather than relying on God.

36. Why did God tell Abraham to sacrifice his son? (22:1) (Faith, Obedience, Sacrifices)

God was giving Abraham an extremely difficult test to confirm his faith and prove his commitment to God.

37. Why did Abraham want Isaac to marry a relative? (24:3–4) (Ancient Practices, Marriage)

Abraham wanted Isaac to marry within his own clan — not someone who worshiped false gods.

38. Why is the story repeated here? (24:34–49) (The Bible)

This part of the story is repeated to stress God's role in the events.

39. How did the marriage become legal? (24:67) (Ancient Practices, Marriage)

The marriage became legal after the two families agreed to the marriage.

40. What is a *concubine*? (25:6) (Ancient Practices, Meanings)

A *concubine* is like a second wife who is more of a servant. Her primary purpose was to bear children.

41. What is a *birthright*? (25:31) (Ancient Practices, Family)

During biblical times special rights were given to the firstborn son, like becoming the leader of the family and inheriting most of the family's land and herds of animals.

42. Why was Isaac's deathbed blessing important? (27:4) (Ancient Practices, Blessings)

Spoken deathbed blessings had legal standing in the ancient Middle East. Jacob knew Isaac could give only one blessing, and Jacob wanted it to secure the birthright he had bought from Esau.

43. Why would God bless Jacob when Jacob lied to get his father's blessing? (27:35) (Blessings, Lying)

God's choice of Jacob was made before he was even born; it was not based on whether he was a good person or not. God's blessings are always unexpected.

44. Are dreams messages from God?

(28:12–15) (Dreams, Talking to God)

They can be. If God speaks to us in a dream, it will correspond to a teaching of the Bible.

45. What was a bridal week? (29:27)

(Ancient Practices, Marriage)

It was a wedding feast that usually lasted seven days.

46. How do we know if a dream is from God? (31:11) (Dreams, Talking to God)

Sometimes God speaks to people in dreams. But not all dreams are from God.

47. Why was Jacob's name changed to Israel? (32:28) (Ancient Practices, Names)

In ancient times, a person's name was changed to mark something important in that person's life. *Israel* means "he struggles with God."

48. Why did Jacob's family have foreign gods? (35:2) (Idols)

Rachel had brought her father's household idols with her, probably as a type of good-luck charm. The captives from Shechem's city probably had their idols with them, too. Jacob's children may have accepted some of the religious beliefs of the pagans in the surrounding cultures.

49. Why did Jacob have so many wives? (35:23–26) (Ancient Practices, Marriage)

The practice of taking many wives (polygamy) was common in the ancient Middle East. It was a sign of wealth and rank. But polygamy goes against God's original plan for marriage to be between one man and one woman.

50. Why list all of Esau's descendants? (36:1–43) (Family, Names)

This genealogy shows how God fulfilled his promise to Sarah to become the mother of nations. (See Genesis 17:16.)

51. What did Joseph's robe look like?

(37:3) (Clothing)

It probably was very bright in color.

52. When Joseph told his brothers his dreams, was he taunting them?

(37:5) (Boasting, Dreams, Prophets)

He may have been proud of his special status, but it's also possible that he was simply acting as a prophet, sharing the truth of God that had been revealed to him.

53. What were widow's clothes? (38:14)

(Ancient Practices, Clothing, Women)

Widows were supposed to dress in a modest fashion. They usually dressed in sackcloth or torn garments. They left their hair unbound and their feet bare.

54. Why did they pay so much attention to dreams? (40:8) (Dreams)

Dreams were thought to come from the gods and should be analyzed to guide people about actions they should take.

55. Why was Joseph able to forgive his brothers? (45:5–7) (Family, Forgiveness)

Joseph knew his brothers' cruel act had accomplished God's purpose: to place him in Egypt where he could save his family from starvation and preserve God's chosen people.

56. Why is this list of names important? (46:8–25) (Family, Names)

Genealogies were important to people in ancient times to record their history and also to show how they were connected to the community.

57. Was it unusual for a grown man to cry so much? (46:29) (Sadness)

▭➤ Joseph seems to have been a sensitive and emotional person. Tears show you are human.

58. Does God use unbelievers to accomplish his will? (47:13–27) (God's Power, Unbelievers)

▭➤ Yes. God is in control of all things and also works through people who have no faith in him.

59. Was Jacob right to put the younger son ahead of the older son? (48:20) (Ancient Practices, Blessings)

▭➤ Yes. He was demonstrating that a blessing is not a right but a gift.

60. How does God care for his people even when things seem to be going wrong? (50) (Blessings, God's Love, Hardship)

☞ Throughout the Bible followers of God experience hardship, pain, or misfortune. But God always provides for his followers. He frequently blesses people who are in difficult situations to allow them to accomplish his purposes.

Exodus

61. Was it morally acceptable for the midwives to lie to Pharaoh? (1:19–20) (Lying)

☞ Because the king's command was evil and contradicted God's law, the midwives were obeying a higher authority: God himself.

62. Was it wrong for Moses' mother to disobey Pharaoh? (2:3) (Obedience)

☞ God wants us to follow the people he has put in place over us. But when these leaders use their power unjustly God wants you to do the right thing in his eyes.

63. Why could the princess adopt Moses if the law said he had to be killed? (2:9–10) (Ancient Practices)

☞ The princess's royal status put her above the law others had to follow — to kill male Hebrew babies. Many people also believe it was a common practice for Egyptian nobility to adopt slaves.

64. What did Moses gain through his adoption by the princess? (Ancient Practices)

☞ First and foremost, Moses gained his life. Second, he received a great education since that was a priority to Egyptians. Third, he was trained in war and leadership.

65. Why did Moses blame God for the trouble? (5:22) (Blame)

He blamed God because speaking in the Lord's name had brought even more trouble for his people.

66. Why did God harden Pharaoh's heart? (7:3) (God's Power)

God hardens a person's heart to accomplish God's purposes, to show his power, and to release the Israelites.

67. Was the water really blood? (7:20) (God's Power, Miracles, Plagues)

Some people think the river was polluted with red dirt during flooding. Others think the water really turned into blood. Both are possible through God.

68. Why did God choose to use frogs as a plague? (8:5) (Animals, Plagues)

God may have chosen frogs because the Egyptians worshiped the goddess Heqt, a frog-headed woman. Pharaoh probably thought Israel was mocking this god.

69. Why did Pharaoh change his mind about letting the Israelites go? (8:15) (Leaders)

Pharaoh wanted the plagues to stop, but he didn't want to look weak by giving in and letting the Israelites go free.

70. Why did God make an exception of Goshen? (8:22) (God's Power, Plagues)

God offered further proof to Pharaoh that it was Israel's God sending the plagues.

71. How badly had Egypt been damaged by the plagues? (10:7)

(Plagues, Punishment)

The plagues devastated the Egyptian economy, people were hurt by boils and biting insects and polluted water, and their religious system was humiliated.

72. Why did Pharaoh say that only the Israelite men could go? (10:11) (Ancient Practices)

Generally it was only men who participated in worship, and Pharaoh probably wanted the women and children to stay behind so he could be assured the men would return.

73. What was the plague of darkness?

(10:21–23) (God's Power, Plagues)

Like the third and sixth plagues, the ninth plague was unannounced. It was possibly caused by a severe sandstorm and caused darkness, insulting the Egyptian sun god Ra.

74. What was the plague on the firstborn sons? (11:4–5) (Ancient Practices, Plagues, Punishment)

Firstborn sons' deaths would have caused great sadness among the people. In addition, judgment on the firstborn represented judgment on the entire community.

75. Why is this last plague remembered with a feast called the Passover? (12:1–28) (Angels, Obedience)

God commanded the Israelites to sprinkle their doors with the blood of a lamb. The angel literally passed over the homes that had this sign on them.

76. Why were the people told to make bread without yeast? (12:15) (Food, Symbols)

The bread without yeast could be made quickly. It also symbolized purity because baking bread with yeast used sour dough.

77. Who was the destroyer? (12:23) (Angels, Punishment)

The destroyer was a type of spirit, perhaps an angel, to bring judgment and punish the Egyptians.

78. Why did all the firstborn sons have to die? (12:29) (Plagues, Punishment)

The final plague of killing all the firstborn sons convinced Pharaoh to free the Israelites — probably because it was such an obvious punishment by God that could not be seen as a coincidence.

79. How many Israelites left Egypt? (12:37) (Israelites)

The total number could have been well over two million people.

80. Did Egyptians go with the Israelites too? (12:38) (Israelites)

☞ Some Egyptians probably wanted to leave the disaster area. Others may have been moved to faith because of God's mighty acts, or had been friends of the Israelites.

81. Why did God wait so long to free his people? (12:40) (Slaves, Waiting)

☞ The Israelites weren't slaves the entire 430 years they were in Egypt. Their slavery probably began about 125 years before they were freed. The important message is that God did not abandon his people. (See Exodus 2:24.)

82. Why did the people consecrate the firstborn males? (13:2) (Ancient Practices)

☞ *Consecrated* means "given to God." God killed the firstborn male in every Egyptian household but spared the Israelites and as a way to show their gratitude and to pay God back for his kindness, animals were killed as substitute sacrifices.

83. Why would the Israelites want to stay in Egypt if they were slaves?

(14:12) (Israelites, Slaves)

They were probably afraid of the unknown and not fully trusting in God.

84. Can a wind push back the sea to make walls of water? (14:21–22)

(Miracles)

A strong hurricane-like wind known as a *sirocco* could displace large amounts of water and cause the land to dry up. But the miracle at the Red Sea was not a natural occurrence. The water was divided on the left and on the right.

85. Is there any historical record of this event? (14:28) (Ancient Practices)

No, except for the account in the Bible. Egyptians did not usually record their defeats in battle.

86. Is dancing a sin? (15:20) (Sin)

God wants everything we do to glorify him. If we are dancing in a way that honors God and not in an inappropriate way, dancing makes God happy.

87. What is *manna*? (16:4, 31) (Food, Meanings)

Manna was the bread God sent at night to feed the Israelites while they were in the desert. It was white and sweet. They called it *manna* because it is like the Hebrew word for "what is it."

88. Why was it wrong for the people to grumble? (16:7) (Complaining, Trust)

The people's grumbling showed that they lacked gratitude and trust for all that God had done for them.

89. What is the *Sabbath*? (16:23) (Sabbath)

The *Sabbath* is a day of rest on the seventh day of the week.

90. Did Jethro worship other gods?

(18:11) (Idols)

☞ He may have worshiped many tribal gods before, but Jethro finally accepted that God is the one and only true God.

91. Would God take away his Promised Land if the Israelites didn't obey him? (19:5) (Promises)

☞ No. God had made an unconditional covenant with Abraham. Although God's blessing may depend on keeping God's law, salvation does not.

92. Do we still need to obey the Ten Commandments? (20) (Commandments, God's Love, Sin)

☞ Yes, they show us what God expects as the right way to behave. They show us how sinful we are, yet God still loves us, and they show us how to live our lives in thankfulness to God for his great love.

93. What does it mean that God is jealous? (20:5) (Jealousy, Meanings)

☞ This means God will not tolerate anything that comes between him and his people.

94 Is saying "Oh my God" wrong even if you aren't trying to use God's name in vain? (20:7) (Sin)

☞ God wants us to honor his name by using it for good and encouraging purposes. When we use it without thinking it means nothing and we are not following his commandments.

95. If God wants us to fear him, why does Moses tell the Israelites not to be afraid? (20:20) (Fear)

☞ To fear God doesn't mean to be afraid of him. It means to have great respect for him and what he does.

96. Why did God require sacrifices?
(20:24) (Ancient Practices, Sacrifices, Sin)

☞ Sacrifices reminded people that God would not ignore sin; someone had to pay the price so that God would forgive the sin. They also showed that the innocent can substitute for the guilty. Sacrifices always involved offering something valuable to God because he deserved the best and served to bring the community together.

97. Why was slavery permitted? (21:2)
(Ancient Practices, Slaves)

☞ Moses allowed this type of slavery as a way to repay debts or to make up for something they did wrong, but with strict rules so it had limits.

98. What was the principle of an "eye for eye, tooth for tooth"? (21:23–25)
(Meanings, Punishment)

☞ This is the idea that the punishment was equal to the harm caused (the same was done to you that you did). This was a balanced approach to punishment.

99. Why is this section entitled "Social Responsibility"? (22:16–31) (The Bible, Worship)

For Israel, all life was rooted in worship, and the quality of people's worship was partly demonstrated by the way they behaved toward other people.

100. How were people expected to act toward their enemies? (23:4–5) (Enemies)

God commanded the Israelites to treat all people with the same consideration. "Love your enemies" (Matthew 5:44).

101. What was the Festival of Harvest? (23:16) (Ancient Practices)

This feast celebrated the first harvested crops and was also called the Festival of Weeks. In the New Testament, this feast was called Pentecost.

102. Why was blood used to confirm the covenant? (24:6–8) (Ancient Practices, Symbols)

The blood on the altar symbolized God's forgiveness. The blood on the people symbolized their promise to follow God.

103. What was the tabernacle? (26:1) (God's Presence, Worship)

The tabernacle was a large structure that was a permanent holy place of worship. It was the place where God showed himself to the Israelites.

104. Why did the rich and poor pay the same offering to the Lord? (30:15) (Money, Offerings)

The point of the ransom was that both rich and poor are equal in God's eyes.

105. Can our prayers cause God to change his mind? (32) (God's Power, Prayer)

God does not change his will just because we pray. God hears our prayers, and sometimes it seems as if he adjusts his plans. But it's important to remember that God is always in charge and always in control.

106. Why did the Israelites want to have a god that they could see? (32:1) (God's Presence, Idols, Israelites)

Ancient people saw an idol as an earthly representation of a god, not as the god itself. The Israelites needed reassurance God was near.

107. Why would future generations be punished for the sins of their fathers and grandfathers? (34:7) (Family, Punishment, Sin)

Families were regarded as a unit, and one person's actions could affect several generations of a family.

108. Why did the people give so freely to build the tabernacle? (36:4–7) (Money, Offerings)

The people may have been impressed with God's power, afraid of his punishment, and inspired by the radiance of Moses after he spoke to God.

109. What was the ark of the covenant? (37) (God's Presence, Symbols)

The ark was a special chestlike box with stone tablets inscribed with the law that God had given to Moses, a jar of manna, and Aaron's rod inside. The ark was a physical symbol of God's glory and his presence with his people.

110. How long did it take to build the tabernacle? (40:17) (Time)

It probably took about six months.

Leviticus

111. Why did God require so many sacrifices from his people?

(1–7) (Forgiveness, Sacrifices)

God required animal sacrifices in order to satisfy the requirements of the covenant and to provide a way for his people to offer thanks and seek forgiveness.

112. How many types of offerings were there? (1:2) (Offerings)

There were five different types of offerings: burnt, grain, fellowship, sin, and guilt. Each offering had a different purpose.

113. Why did sacrifices have to be made for unintentional sins? (4:2) (Sacrifice, Sin)

In this context *unintentional* means "wandering away." This type of sin was made out of weakness of character rather than active rebellion.

114. Why were the people guilty for a priest's sin? (4:3) (Guilt, Priests, Sin)

In the Old Testament, the priest represented the people to God. If he was not pure, he became a flawed representative.

115. What were sin offerings? (4:1–35) (Ancient Practices, Offerings, Sin)

Sin offerings covered many sins and were made for the whole congregation on all of the feast days, especially on the Day of Atonement.

116. How could someone take an oath and not know it? (5:4) (Oaths)

Taking an oath without knowing it means taking an oath before thinking about the consequences of breaking it.

117. What was wrong with eating blood? (7:26–27) (Ancient Practices, Forgiveness, Offerings)

☞ Blood was used in offerings to ask for forgiveness.

118. Why was Aaron, who was sinful, made a high priest? (8:30) (Priests, Sin)

☞ Every person sins and no one is perfect so even though Aaron made the golden calf, he also helped Moses.

119. What was the difference between clean and unclean foods? (11:1–47) (Cleanliness, Food)

☞ The Bible does not give the answer, but these food laws helped the Israelites eat a healthy diet and maintain their identity as his holy covenant people.

120. Why would giving birth make a woman ceremonially unclean? (12:1–5) (Cleanliness, Women)

☞ The ancient Israelites thought the blood associated with birth was unclean.

121. Why did God give these laws about personal cleanliness? (15:1–33)

(Cleanliness)

Not only did these laws help keep the people clean and help prevent sickness, they were also a way for God to differentiate his people from others.

122. Why were natural functions considered unclean? (15:16–24)

(Cleanliness)

God created us so there is nothing sinful about the way our bodies function. However, God gave a set of rules about what was considered unclean in order to protect people from getting sick and the law required cleansing from any sort of bodily discharge.

123. Why could being close to God cause Aaron to die? (16:2) (Death, God's Power)

Unless Aaron was properly prepared, God's glory in the Most Holy Place would kill him.

124. Why is it specifically blood that atones for sin? (17:11) (Sacrifices, Sin)

Blood is necessary for life. When the animal's blood was shed, it was paying the price for the sinner with its life.

125. Why are there so many rules that start with "Do not"? (18:7–24) (Commandments)

By using the negative language, the rules clearly state the expected correct behavior.

126. Does God expect his followers to be perfect? (19:2) (Commandments, Perfection)

God doesn't expect them to be perfect, but he expects them to be holy and follow God's commandments.

127. Why were there laws about hairstyles and tattoos? (19:27–28)
(Pagan Practices)

The rules were meant to keep the Israelites from copying rituals performed by pagans that showed disrespect for God.

128. Is it a sin to get a tattoo? (19:28) (Pagan Practices, Sin)

The laws of the Old Testament had rules against tattoos because they were connected with pagan rituals. God wants you to respect your body and think twice before you permanently mark it.

129. What was the difference between a freewill offering and a vow? (22:23)
(Offerings, Vows)

Unlike a vow that was based on a preexisting promise, a freewill offering was voluntary.

130. Is it really so bad to swear? (24)
(Language)

Yes, when swearing is using God's name in a wrong way by cursing or without respect it is offensive to God, and it harms our Christian witness.

131. Why did God permit slavery of the Canaanites? (25:44–46) (God's Power, Slaves)

God would not allow his own people to be ruled over as slaves, but he permitted slaves to be bought from the pagan nations around them. God modified the custom of slavery and improved the lives of slaves by setting up restrictions the Israelites were to follow.

132. What does it mean that God had a dwelling place among the people?
(26:11) (God's Presence)

God's presence was with the Israelites in a special way in the tabernacle, which means *dwelling place*.

133. Are afflictions always punishment from God? (26:24) (Hardship, Punishment)

Afflictions are not punishment from God, but when they happen, God may use them as a way to test his people and strengthen their faith.

134. What is an uncircumcised heart? (26:41) (Sin, Symbols)

This is a figurative way to talk about the sinful hearts of the people.

135. Why were men worth more than women and the middle-aged worth more than the elderly? (27:3–8) (Priests, Women)

The priests expected more hard work from middle-aged men.

Numbers

136. How did God speak to Moses? (1:1)
(Talking to God)

▷ At times Moses seemed to have actually heard the voice of God. At other times he may have experienced an inner conversation or conviction.

137. What were banners and standards?
(2:2) (Ancient Practices)

▷ Each tribe had its own banner, and each group of three tribes had its own standard. These were like flags that were carried into battle.

138. Why would God kill people for looking at the holy things? (4:20)
(Death, God's Power)

▷ Disrespect of spiritual things would not be tolerated.

139. Why were people with skin diseases or discharges banished from the camp? (5:2–3) (Cleanliness, Sickness)

👉 Skin diseases and discharges made the camp ceremonially unclean. Banishment protected the rest of the camp.

140. Why wasn't there a test for unfaithfulness for men? (5:31) (Ancient Practices, Marriage)

👉 Women typically didn't beat their husbands for adultery, so they didn't need the same kind of laws for protection.

141. Why did God impose age restrictions on those who served as priests? (8:24–25) (Age, Priests)

👉 A minimum age helped ensure the worker would be mature enough to handle the tasks and made sure the priest was in good physical shape.

142. Why did the Israelites' complaints make the Lord angry? (11:1) (Anger, Complaining, Israelites)

He was angry because they were ungrateful and did not have faith in him.

143. Does God punish children for what their parents do? (14) (Family, Punishment)

Sin has consequences that sometimes carry on through the generations. But just because someone suffers does not mean that God is directly punishing that person for his or her sin or the sin of the parents.

144. Who decided whether a sin was intentional or not? (15:22–29) (Priests, Sin)

A person would talk to the priest about his or her sin, and the priest would decide whether it was due to weakness or choosing to rebel against God.

145. Does God forgive unintentional sins more easily than intentional?

(15:22–29) (Forgiveness, Sin)

☞ God sees all sins as the same, through Jesus we are forgiven equally for all of our sins, whether intentional or not.

146. Why did sacrifices have to be made for unintentional sins? (15:22–29)

(Sacrifices, Sin)

☞ The Israelites believed there was guilt associated with any sin, and they had to get rid of the guilt.

147. Why did people wear tassels to help them obey God's laws?

(15:38–40) (Clothing, The Law)

☞ All Jews wore tassels on their clothing in order to remind themselves of their promise to be faithful to God's commands, similar to the way we wear WWJD? bracelets to remind ourselves to follow Jesus' example.

148. Why was being a priest considered a gift? (18:7) (Priests)

Just like God gives us special gifts to do certain things, priests were chosen based on their special relationship with God and had a gift to be able to save the people from God's anger.

149. Why were the third and seventh days special? (19:12) (Symbols)

The numbers three and seven symbolize fullness or completeness.

150. Why does complaining make God so angry? (21:5–6) (Complaining)

When people complain, they show disrespect, disobedience, and lack of trust in God.

151. What is an *oracle*? (23:1–24:25) (Meanings)

The *oracle* that the Bible is referring to is an announcement or message from God.

152. What is the meaning of "God is not human, that he should lie"? (23:19) (Meanings)

▭➤ God is described as being completely truthful.

153. Why did God punish people who didn't worship Baal? (25:9) (Idols, Punishment)

▭➤ Because the sin was the responsibility of the community, the plague killed people throughout the community.

154. How did the Israelites know when a new month started? (28:11) (Israelites, Time)

▭➤ The Hebrews based their calendar system on the phases of the moon.

155. How were the Israelites supposed to deny themselves? (29:7) (Ancient Practices, Israelites)

☐☞ On the Day of Atonement the people denied themselves by not eating.

156. Why were the Israelites sometimes allowed to keep plunder from battles? (31:9) (Ancient Practices, Battles, Israelites)

☐☞ Because God told them to take the Midianites' wealth.

157. What did Moses mean when he said, "Your sin will find you out"? (32:23) (Meanings)

☐☞ Moses agreed to the proposal, but he warned them to keep their promise to help the rest of the Israelites conquer the land of Canaan. If the Reubenites and Gadites didn't keep their word to Moses, he warned there would be severe penalties.

158. Did all women have to marry within their own tribe? (36:3) (Ancient Practices, Marriage, Women)

▭➤ No, only women who inherited land had to marry within their own tribe.

Deuteronomy

159. Why wouldn't God accept the people's repentance? (1:45) (Repentance)

▭➤ The people weren't sincere with their repentance. They were sorry, but God was not impressed by this show of repentance that came too late.

160. If God was mad at the Israelites, why did he watch over them while they were being punished? (2:7) (God's Love, Punishment)

▭➤ The Israelites had displeased God, but that didn't mean he didn't still love them. By watching over the Israelites, God took care of them; and after 40 years, God knew they'd learned to trust him.

161. Why were some nations spared and others defeated? (2:24) (Punishment)

God dealt with each nation differently. To some he showed his mercy, while others became tools of punishment toward Israel.

162. Why would the Israelites be tempted to worship idols? (4:15–19) (Idols, Israelites, Worship)

They may have been tempted to worship something they could see and not just hear occasionally.

163. Why did God choose the Israelites over anyone else to be his people?

(4:33) (Israelites)

It wasn't because they were special or deserved God's favor, but through God's timing, the Israelites were chosen to bring God's blessings to the world.

164. What did it mean to observe the Sabbath? (5) (Meanings, Sabbath)

The Sabbath, or seventh day of the week, was set aside as a day which people were to keep as holy by not doing any work and experience physical, mental, and spiritual restoration. (See Mark 2:27.)

165. Must Christians still obey the Ten Commandments? (5:6–21) (Christians, Commandments, Obedience)

Yes. They show what God expects as correct behavior and how sinful we are. But they are also important because they show Christians how to live their lives in thankfulness to God for his great love.

166. Why do the commandments include consequences for future generations? (5:9–10) (Ancient Practices, Commandments)

☞ This is like the language used in ancient treaties. If people broke the treaty, the effects would be felt by entire families — even into future generations. If the people obeyed the treaty, they would be rewarded.

167. What does it mean that "man does not live on bread alone"?

(8:3) (Meanings)

☞ God's truths are even more important than food.

168. Did Moses' prayer change God's mind? (9:25–29) (God's Power, Prayer)

No one is sure. This may be a way of explaining God's actions in human terms rather than actually meaning that Moses changed God's mind.

169. Why were these commands about worship given first? (12:4–7) (Commandments, Worship)

This shows the importance of establishing permanent practices of worship as the Israelites get settled in the new land.

170. What is a tithe? (12:17) (Offerings)

Here a *tithe* (a tenth) referred to giving one-tenth of one's crops and livestock to the Lord.

171. Why would God warn his people about sacrificing their children? (12:31) (Pagan Practices, Sacrifices)

☞ Pagan worship sometimes included human sacrifices, even sacrifices of children. God wanted his people to completely avoid these practices that were designed to win favor with pagan gods.

172. Why did God test his people?
(13:3) (Faith)

☞ Testing them taught them what they needed to know about themselves, and showed whether they would remain faithful and obedient to God.

173. Did the Israelites have no religious freedom? (13:5) (Free Will, Israelites)

☞ The Israelites always had the freedom to choose, but if they rejected God, they would pay for their actions. They had a unique relationship with the Lord, and if they rejected God, they were breaking a promise they had made.

174. Do Jews today still follow these food laws? (14:3–21) (Food, Jewish Practices)

Kosher laws are still followed by Orthodox Jews, but not all Jews.

175. What should a believer's attitude be toward the poor? (15:11) (Believers, Generosity, The Poor)

God's command is to be generous in helping those who are poor.

176. Is fortunetelling always wrong? (18:9–13) (Pagan Practices)

Yes. Even if this is just done as a game or for fun, it still is wrong because it goes against God's commandments and because it denies that God alone can see into the future.

177. How could people tell if a message was from a false prophet? (18:21–22)
(Prophets)

If a prophecy contradicted God's will or proved wrong, it must have come from a false prophet.

178. Why would God approve of taking women and children as plunder?
(20:14) (Ancient Practices, Battles)

It was common at that time to take prisoners of war. But God expected Israel to treat these people fairly.

179. Why is there a note about saving the trees? (20:19) (Nature)

They were told to save the trees that could support them with food.

180. Why would a girl have to marry a man who raped her? (22:29) (Ancient Practices, Marriage, Women)

Her father could not get the full marriage price for her, so this law forced the man to pay the price for something he tried to take without obligation.

181. Was divorce something that God allowed? (24:1–4) (Marriage)

God permitted divorce in some circumstances, but divorce was uncommon among the Hebrews.

182. Does God see sins that are done secretly? (27:15, 24) (Sin)

Yes. God sees all sins — even the ones done secretly.

183. Why would it please God to destroy Israel? (28:63) (Punishment, Sin)

God did not want to punish his people, but he would make sure justice was done.

184. Does God ever want us to feel anxious? (28:65–67) (Fear, Worry)

Anxiety is a natural emotion, but it isn't a punishment from God. God provides the comfort we need through the Bible. When we're afraid or worried, we can pray to God and ask for his help, and other Christians can help us by listening to our concerns, comforting us, and praying with us.

185. Was there a sin that God would not forgive? (29:18–20) (Forgiveness, Sin)

A person who turned away from God to worship pagan gods would not be forgiven.

186. What is the difference between heart and soul? (30:6) (Differences)

☞ *Heart* often meant the mind or intellect, and *soul* usually meant human desire or will. God wants us to love him with both our heart and our soul.

187. Was it possible to perfectly obey the Old Testament law? (30:11) (The Law, Perfection, Sin)

☞ No. Sin kept people from keeping God's law perfectly. The only one who was ever able to obey the law without sin was Jesus.

188. What did it mean to choose life? (30:19–20) (Life, Meanings)

☞ When the Israelites chose to follow the Lord and his laws, their lives would become filled with blessings.

189. Why would God become jealous?
(32:21) (Jealousy)

God expected his people to worship only him.

190. Did God expect those who served him to completely ignore their families? **(33:9)** (Family)

No, this is an example of exaggeration to emphasize total commitment to God's law.

191. Why was Israel so blessed? **(33:29)**
(Blessings, Israelites)

They were blessed because God chose them to be a model of his love to the rest of the world.

192. How old was Moses when he died?
(34:7) (Age, Death)

He was 120 years old, but still very strong and vital.

Joshua

193. Did God really speak out loud to Joshua? (1:1) (Talking to God)

We aren't sure. But we do know he communicated directly with Joshua, giving instructions for entering the Promised Land.

194. Would God ever want someone to disobey one of his commandments?

(2) (Commandments)

God is righteous, and he expects his people to obey the laws that he has given. But there are situations when two of God's laws come into conflict. When this happens, it is important to prayerfully ask for wisdom about what to do.

195. Why would a city have its own king? (2:2) (Ancient Practices, Leaders)

The major cities in Canaan were actually small kingdoms, and each one was ruled by its own king.

196. What type of calendar did the Israelites use? (4:9) (Israelites, Time)

Israel used two calendars: one sacred (based on religious holidays), and one agricultural (based on farming practices).

197. Why did God tell us not to kill, yet the Old Testament is full of stories about battles? (6) (Battles, Commandments)

In the Bible God often commanded his people to go to war against other countries that opposed them because God was trying to accomplish something good.

198. Why did God speak as if the victory had already happened? (6:2) (Battles, God's Power)

God knew the outcome, and the Israelites were guaranteed the victory.

199. Why did God tell the Israelites to march around the city? (6:3) (Ancient Practices, Battles)

In ancient times, circling a city was a common practice before attacking.

200. How could confessing sin give glory to God? (7:19) (Sin)

By confessing sin, the sinner acknowledged that what they did was wrong and that God was ultimately right.

201. Is it wrong to break a promise? (9:19) (Promises)

When you make a promise, it is your responsibility to keep that promise and be an example of how God treats promises — even if you don't want to keep your promise or were tricked into that promise.

202. Were there ever more books in the Bible? (10:13) (The Bible)

The Bible mentions 28 other books, many of which are missing.

203. Why did the Israelites leave some pagan peoples undefeated? (11:22–23) (Battles, Israelites)

They were probably tired of fighting and stopped before all of the people were defeated.

204. Did women have many rights? (17:3–4) (Women)

Women had relatively few rights compared to today.

Judges

205. What pattern of behavior took place during the time of the judges? (2) (Time)

The pattern had four parts. First, the Israelites would fall away from God. Second, God would be angry with the Israelites and punish them. Third, the Israelites would ask God to deliver them from the other tribes. Finally, God would send a judge who would deliver them.

206. What was the angel of the Lord? (2:1, 4) (Angels)

Some think this was God in human form. Others think that it was an angel, a spirit sent, or perhaps a prophet or a priest sent by God.

207. How could a whole generation of Israelites not know the Lord? (2:10)

(Israelites)

The Israelites became too comfortable with their Canaanite neighbors' beliefs and gradually forgot about God.

208. Why did the people need judges to help them stay faithful to God? (2:19)

(Faith, Leaders, Pagan Practices)

Without strong leadership, the people of Israel stopped following the Lord and adopted pagan practices.

209. How did a woman become a judge in this male-dominated society?

(4:4) (Ancient Practices, Women)

Deborah probably had strong leadership abilities, and God blessed her for her trust in him.

210. Why did the Israelites keep repeating the same mistakes? (10:6)
(Idols, Israelites)

They seemed unable to resist the temptation to worship false gods, and might have thought that God would always save them.

211. Why did the elders pick an outcast to lead them? (11:4–6) (Leaders)

Jephthah had shown that he was an effective leader, so when no one else volunteered to be leader at Mizpah, the elders recruited him.

212. What was a Nazirite? (13:5) (Ancient Practices, Meanings)

A *Nazirite* was a person who made a special vow to the Lord that lasted 30 days or even a lifetime. A Nazirite could not eat or drink grape products, cut his or her hair, or go near a dead body.

213. How was the angel's name beyond understanding? (13:18) (Angels)

He was not an ordinary angel, but somehow linked to God himself. No words we have will ever be good enough to describe God.

214. Did God cause Samson to break a commandment? (14:4) (Commandments)

No. God never wants his people to disobey his rules. Samson was responsible for his own actions.

215. Can God use sinful people for his purposes? (15) (God's Power, Sin)

God can use anyone to accomplish his purposes, but what he wants is our love and devotion.

216. Did Samson's hair make him strong? (16:20) (Ancient Practices)

Samson lost his strength not because his hair was short, but because he had broken his vows to God as a Nazirite.

217. Did the Lord leave Samson permanently? (16:20) (Forgiveness)

No. God's love for Samson continued even though Samson had broken his vows.

218. Why did the Israelites lose so many people after receiving guidance from God? (20:18–25) (Battles, Israelites)

They did not rely entirely on God but also trusted in their own abilities to give them victory. They should have put their faith in God alone.

Ruth

219. Was Ruth being disloyal to her own family and people? (1) (Faith)

▭▸ No, Ruth's decision to leave with Naomi proved her strong faith in the God of Israel.

220. Is it the responsibility of Christians to care for the poor? (2) (Christians, Generosity, The Poor)

▭▸ The Bible strongly emphasizes the need for Christians to be generous to those who are homeless, hungry, or hurting.

221. Why was Ruth allowed to take grain from other people's fields? (2:2) (Jewish Practices)

▭▸ The law gave foreigners, widows, and orphans the right to take what was left after the main harvest was completed.

222. Is it okay to get remarried? (4:10)

(Marriage)

God doesn't want people to take marriage lightly and get divorced in order to marry someone else. However, he does want his followers to be taken care of, and many widows in the Bible get remarried.

1 Samuel

223. Did Hannah blame God for not being able to have children?

(1:5) (Blame, Faith, Trust)

No, she realized that God was ultimately in control of everything.

224. Does God make some people poor?

(2:7) (The Poor, Punishment)

God is just and brings some people up and others down as punishment for their sins.

225. Why did the people want the ark of the covenant sent back to Israel?
(5:11) (God's Power)

The people realized that after three towns had been struck by tumors, God must be the source of the disease.

226. Why did the Israelites want a king if they had God? (8:5–18) (Israelites, Leaders)

They wanted to be like the other nations; even though Samuel warned them that having a king meant they would be slaves to their king's demands.

227. What did Samuel warn that a king would do to them? (8:11–18) (Leaders)

Samuel warned that they would become like slaves to a human king and his demands.

228. Why did Saul say he was not worthy to serve? (9:21) (Leaders)

This was a common response from the men God chose to serve in leadership roles. When God made Saul king, he continued his pattern of selecting leaders who seemed the least qualified.

229. What kinds of weapons did Israelites use? (13:22) (Battles, Leaders)

Axes, sickles, goads (a long pointed stick), slingshots, and bows and arrows.

230. Is God pleased more by obedience or sacrifices? (15:20–22) (Obedience, Sacrifices)

God would rather his people be obedient to him and trust him than to make sacrifices to him.

231. Could Saul be forgiven for his sin? (15:25–26) (Forgiveness, Punishment)

Yes. God punished Saul and his descendants but that does not mean that God didn't forgive him.

232. How could an evil spirit be from God? (16:14) (Evil Spirits)

The term *evil spirit* could also mean "a troubling or injurious spirit." Saul may have been depressed because the Lord had left him.

233. How old was David when he fought Goliath? (17:33) (Age)

Probably around 17 or 18 years old.

234. Why would David have an idol in his house? (19:13) (Idols, Symbols)

Michal may have kept the idol secretly. Or it was a cultural symbol, not an actual idol that was worshiped.

235. How could Jonathan not have known about his father's plan to kill David? (20:9) (Family, Friendship)

☐➤ Saul knew his son and David were great friends, so he would not have told him. Saul had also promised not to kill David, and Jonathan no doubt believed his father.

236. What did it mean to cut off the corner of someone's robe? (24:4) (Meanings)

☐➤ During that time, cutting off the corner of someone's robe was a symbol of disloyalty and rebellion.

237. Why did David still refer to Saul as "the LORD's anointed"? (26:9) (Names)

☐➤ David had respect for the office in spite of the actions of the person who held it.

238. Can spirits be called from the dead?
(28) (Pagan Practices)

It isn't clear whether it was the spirit of Samuel or an evil spirit that took the form of Samuel. But believers should seek God's will through prayer and Scripture reading and should not dabble in the realm of the spirit world.

239. Can a person who commits suicide go to heaven? (31) (Death, Heaven, Suicide)

It's easy to conclude that if an unbeliever commits suicide, then he or she will not be saved. But the Bible says nothing about suicide keeping a believer out of heaven. (See Romans 8:38 – 39.)

240. What does it mean to fast? (31:13)
(Food, Meanings, Mourning, Repentance)

Fasting means going without food for a period of time, and was often done as an act of mourning, repentance, or preparation.

2 Samuel

241. Why did David and his men mourn the death of Saul, their enemy?

(1:12) (Death, Enemies, Mourning)

It makes sense that David would be sad about his best friend Jonathan's death. And even though Saul was corrupt, the death of a king would mean difficult times lay ahead for Israel.

242. Why did David say that Jonathan's love was "more wonderful than that of women"? (1:26) (Love, Women)

Men in that time typically viewed women as inferiors and regarded wives as possessions.

243. What was *sackcloth*? (3:31) (Ancient Practices, Clothing, Mourning)

The English word *sackcloth* comes from the Hebrew word *sak*, which refers to a coarse cloth, dark in color. It was worn by mourners and sometimes by prophets. This uncomfortable garment was often worn next to the skin.

244. Why did David dance? (6:14) (Ancient Practices)

☞ Dance was considered an important part of religious ceremonies in ancient Israel.

245. Why did they shave half of each man's beard and cut off their garments? (10:4–6) (Ancient Practices, Clothing, Punishment)

☞ Both were extremely embarrassing acts in the ancient world. Beards were usually only shaved as a sign of mourning or self-humiliation. And public nakedness was considered shameful.

246. Why was there a season for war?

(11:1) (Battles)

⬜➤ David's army was not a year-round army. The men who served as soldiers were also farmers, so during planting and harvesting seasons they did not serve as soldiers.

247. How should we act when someone points out that we have sinned?

(12) (Repentance, Sin)

⬜➤ We should show sincere repentance like David did when he sinned.

248. What did David mean when he said, "I will go to him?" (12:23) (Death, Meanings)

⬜➤ David knew that his son would never come back to him, but he took comfort knowing that after David died they would be reunited.

249. Why was covering the head a sign of sorrow? (15:30) (Ancient Practices, Sadness)

Covering the head was an embarrassing show of a loss of freedom because in Israel, an uncovered head was a sign of a man's integrity and freedom before God.

250. How could David say he was "blameless"? (22:24) (Blame, Forgiveness, Sin)

This song was written long before David's sin with Bathsheba and murder of Uriah. But even if it had been written afterward, God had forgiven David.

251. Why does David call God "my Rock"? (22:47) (God's Power, Names)

David recognized that true security was found only in the Lord.

1 Kings

252. What is the difference between an independent prophet and an official prophet? (1:9–10) (Differences, Prophets)

Independent prophets worked on their own, like Elijah; and official prophets served in the king's court, like Nathan.

253. Why was worshiping at the high places wrong? (3:3) (Pagan Practices, Worship)

The high places were originally where the Canaanites had worshiped their gods. The Israelites often sinned by mixing their worship of God with worship of pagan gods.

254. Why did Solomon call himself "a little child"? (3:7–9) (Age, Leaders)

At 20, Solomon did not have much experience or knowledge as a king, and he asked God to give him wisdom.

255. What kind of wisdom was Solomon given? (4:29–34) (Wisdom)

☞ Solomon had asked for discernment so he could decide between right and wrong in order to govern fairly.

256. Why did Solomon spend more time building his palace than he did the temple? (6:38–7:1) (Material Possessions, The Temple)

☞ His priorities were not right. Solomon's love for material possessions was starting to outweigh his love for the Lord.

257. Why were statues of bulls allowed in the temple? (7:25) (God's Power, Idols, The Temple)

☞ These bulls were not idols. They were there to serve as a reminder of God's power and not in any way associated with the pagan god Baal.

258. Was there a difference between a temple for God and a temple for his "Name"? (8:27–29) (God's Presence, Names, The Temple)

Yes. No building can ever contain all of God's glory. So Solomon dedicated the temple to God's name, knowing that God would be present in the temple in a special way.

259. Why is it necessary for God to turn people's hearts toward himself? (8:58) (God's Power, Sin)

Because of sin, people don't automatically turn toward God.

260. What was Solomon's mistake? (11:1–4) (Commandments, Marriage, Sin)

Solomon disobeyed God's advice by marrying many wives (Deut. 17:17), and he ignored the commandment not to marry pagan women. Solomon's actions disregarded God's laws.

261. How was David a man whose heart was "fully devoted to the LORD"?

(11:4) (Repentance)

☐ Even though David committed many sins, he seemed to always be truly remorseful when he did wrong, and never worshiped idols.

262. Why would anyone be willing to become a false priest? (13:33) (Priests, Prophecies, Sin)

☐ Jeroboam's priests wanted money and power. They did not fear the prophecy that had been given against false priests.

263. Why would God use an evil man like Baasha to accomplish his purposes? (15:34) (God's Power, Unbelievers)

☐ God can do anything, including turning evil intended for selfish gain into a good deed.

264. If I'm depressed, does that mean I don't have enough faith? (19)

(Depression, Faith, Meanings)

👉 No. Feeling sad or depressed is not a sign of spiritual weakness or lack of faith. It is a combination of difficult circumstances along with chemical reactions in the brain. We should seek help through prayer, advice from counselors and pastors, and maybe seek medical help.

265. Why wasn't God in the wind, earthquake, or fire? (19:11–13) (God's Power, Nature)

👉 God instead revealed himself in something common and not all that spectacular: a gentle whisper.

266. Does God approve of lying? (22:20–22)

(Lying)

👉 No, but God allowed the 400 false prophets to speak lies. He used their lies to accomplish his purpose. God gave Ahab a choice — believe the lies or believe the truth.

2 Kings

267. Why did Joram blame God for his troubles? (3:10) (Blame, Hardship)

⬜➤ The three kings did not pray or consult a prophet for advice until after they were in deep trouble.

268. Does God punish people by sending diseases like leprosy or AIDS? (5) (Punishment, Sickness)

⬜➤ If someone we know becomes ill or contracts a disease, we should not think God is punishing that person. There are many diseases today that people can contract, and we should never assume that they are a curse or punishment from God. But there are some behaviors that can contribute to some illnesses so it is important to choose a healthy lifestyle.

269. Why would leprosy strike someone God favored? (5:1) (God's Power, Sickness)

Even when God uses people for good purposes, he doesn't necessarily solve all of their problems. In Naaman's case, his illness showed him how a powerful God can do anything.

270. Why did the king wear sackcloth under his clothes? (6:30) (Ancient Practices, Clothing, Repentance, Sadness)

He was wearing it as a sign of sorrow or repentance. By hiding the sackcloth under his royal robes, it's possible the king wanted to maintain a sense of dignity in front of his people.

271. Why were assassins allowed to become kings? (15:10, 14) (Leaders, Murder)

There was generally no one to stop an assassin who took the throne by force, especially if the murderer had an army backing him up.

272. Why would they kill unborn babies? (15:16) (Battles, Murder)

This brutal act was probably meant to keep babies from growing up to be warriors and maintain control over conquered people.

273. Why did it matter where the people worshiped God? (18:22) (Sacrifices, Worship)

God did not approve of people worshiping him and pagan gods at the same time. God's people could pray anywhere, but sacrifices could only be offered in Jerusalem.

274. Was the Hebrew language well-known? (18:26–28) (Language)

Aramaic had become the international language of the Middle East. It was the language used for diplomacy and commerce.

275. Do miracles still happen today?

(20) (God's Power, Miracles)

Yes. God can do miracles today, but Christians have an obligation to seek ordinary means of accomplishing things such as maintaining good health and seeking medical care rather than relying on miracles. When prayers are answered and miracles seem to occur, we should give thanks to God.

276. Is it okay to ask God for a sign?

(20:8–11) (Talking to God)

Yes, it is good to pray and ask God what to do when you're confused, but God won't always give you a sign in the way you expect.

277. In what way were the Israelites more evil than the nations before them? (21:9) (Idols, Israelites)

They were God's chosen people, yet they rejected the covenant and worshiped idols and not God alone.

278. How common were women prophets in Judah? (22:14) (Prophets, Women)

They were not that common, but female prophets were highly respected.

279. Why were the poor left behind? (24:14) (The Poor)

Babylon wanted to take only those with skills or talents. The poor, who lacked skills and education, would be a drain on Babylon's economy.

1 Chronicles

280. Why does the Bible include so many lists of names? (1) (Family, Names)

Genealogies reminded the people of how God had cared for them throughout their history. Many of the genealogies in the Bible trace the roots of God's people back to Abraham, Isaac, and Jacob and reminded the people of God's promises to those individuals and the way God had carried out those promises throughout history.

281. Why were these genealogies recorded? (1:1–9:44) (Family, God's Power)

The genealogies served as a brief history to show that the Israel of the restoration stood at the center of God's plan from the very beginning, starting with Adam.

282. Why are only sons listed? (1:5) (Ancient Practices)

The Israelites lived in a patriarchal culture where men held the power.

283. What is the difference between a *chief* and a *king*? (1:51) (Differences, Leaders)

▭➤ Chiefs worked under the king. There could be more than one chief, but only one king.

284. What is the difference between *families* and *clans*? (2:52–55) (Family)

▭➤ The word *clan* is sometimes used to describe a larger group of relatives than *family*, but for the most part, they mean the same thing.

285. What were the rights and responsibilities of a firstborn son? (5:1) (Ancient Practices, Family)

▭➤ The firstborn son typically was assigned clan leadership. He became head of the family, inherited more than his brothers, was in charge of his younger siblings, and he was responsible for his mother and unmarried sisters. He also received the covenant blessing.

286. How did Saul's unfaithfulness cause his death? (10:13) (Death, Faith)

Saul's sins did not immediately cause him to die, but the many times he turned away from the Lord, including his meeting with the medium at Endor, led to his death.

287. How was David's army like the army of God? (12:22) (Blessings)

This description implies that God gave his blessing to David and his very large army.

288. Did the ark have special powers? (13) (God's Presence, Symbols)

The ark was an extremely important symbol of God's presence among his people. It did not have magical power, but the fact that God was present was magical.

289. Why was Michal so angry about David's dancing? (15:29) (Anger, Leaders)

☐➤ Michal apparently felt it was undignified for a king to remove his royal robe in order to dance before the ark where his subjects could see him.

290. Why did God decide to change his dwelling from the tabernacle to a temple? (17:5–6, 12) (The Temple)

☐➤ The tabernacle had been designed to be portable as the Israelites traveled through the desert and began to settle in the Promised Land, but the temple would be a permanent structure.

291. Why did David cripple most of the horses that were captured? (18:4)
(Battles, Faith)

☐➤ David knew God wanted the people to trust in God rather than in horses and chariots.

292. What was a seer? (21:9) (Meanings)

☐➤ A *seer* was the same as a prophet — both were messengers from God to his people.

293. Why would the Lord be grieved by something he had ordered?

(21:15) (Punishment, Sadness, Suffering)

⬜➤ God was troubled when his people suffered.

294. Was it unusual to treat the youngest and the oldest son the same? (24:31) (Age, Ancient Practices, Family)

⬜➤ Yes. According to the inheritance laws, the firstborn inherited a double portion of his father's possessions.

295. How could a father transfer the rights of a firstborn? (26:10) (Ancient Practices, Family)

⬜➤ The rights of a firstborn could be given to another son if the older son had shown he was undeserving.

296. **How was the hand of the Lord on David?** (28:19) (The Bible, God's Power, Leaders)

God inspired David to write these things, just as God inspired other writers of the Bible.

297. **What does it mean that God tests the heart?** (29:17) (God's Power, Meanings)

God sees beneath the surface and knows people's motives.

2 Chronicles

298. **Can the Bible exaggerate and still be considered true?** (1) (The Bible, Truth)

It is important to understand the way the Bible uses many literary devices and figures of speech, such as hyperbole, simile, and metaphor. Understanding those techniques will help us to understand the truth the author is trying to get across in a poetic or figurative way.

299. Why did Solomon build the Temple on Mount Moriah? (3:1) (Biblical Places)

This location was special. It was the site of an altar that David built to God, asking him to stop a plague. It was also where Abraham showed his great faith by almost sacrificing his own son.

300. Why were pomegranates used in the decoration of the Temple? (4:13) (The Temple)

People associated pomegranates with beauty. They symbolized God's beauty during worship.

301. Why did Solomon kneel when he prayed? (6:13) (Leaders, Prayer)

As the king, Solomon was in the position of highest authority; however, when he knelt down, Solomon publicly acknowledged that even he was below God. God is the ultimate authority.

302. Why was the temple called God's "resting place"? (6:41) (God's Presence, The Temple)

⬜➤ The temple was where God allowed his people to build a permanent place to worship him.

303. How long would it take to offer 142,000 sacrifices? (7:5) (Ancient Practices, Sacrifices, Time)

⬜➤ Probably around two weeks, which was the time the festival lasted.

304. Why did the Queen of Sheba want to test Solomon's wisdom? (9:1) (Wisdom)

⬜➤ The queen knew there must be a connection between his wisdom and the God he served. She wanted to witness the gift firsthand.

305. What was a covenant of salt? (13:5)
(Ancient Practices, Food)

A covenant of salt probably symbolized that the covenant would last forever since salt is a preservative.

306. How did people learn about God before these teachers came? (17:7–9)
(The Law, Priests, Prophets)

Typically people would visit prophets or priests to learn about the government's laws and moral obligations.

307. Why was an international treaty settled with a wedding? (18:1) (Ancient Practices, Marriage, Politics)

This was common in ancient times. Marriage would mean that breaking the treaty could cause the king personal problems, as well as political.

308. Was it common for kings to pray publicly? (20:5–12) (Leaders, Prayer)

⬜➔ David, Solomon, and Josiah all prayed publicly at special occasions.

309. How does God reward obedience?
(20:30) (Obedience)

⬜➔ God grants victories for those who are obedient and righteous, but the wicked experience defeat.

310. Why were the weapons kept in the temple? (23:9) (The Temple)

⬜➔ Weapons were stored in the temple so people could see them and constantly be reminded of how God helped them conquer their enemies.

311. How could the priests tell who was clean and unclean? (23:19) (Cleanliness, Priests)

⬜➔ The doorkeepers probably stopped everyone entering the temple and reminded them that they had to be ceremonially clean in order to enter.

312. How much were soldiers paid?

(25:6) (Battles, Money)

The usual rate was not much — about three shekels of silver each (a bit more than an ounce). Soldiers were given food and supplies though, and were able to claim the loot they took in battles.

313. What was the fear of God? (26:5) (Fear)

The fear of God meant Uzziah had extreme respect for God, not that he was afraid.

314. What were these corrupt practices?

(27:2) (Idols)

The people continued to worship pagan gods instead of exclusively worshiping the one true God.

315. Why is the number seven so special in the Bible? (29:21) (Perfection, Symbols)

Seven represents perfection and rest. It is the number of days God took to create the world.

316. How could the king command people to worship God? (29:30) (Leaders, Worship)

In ancient cultures, people accepted direction such as this from their leaders.

317. What was the regular time for Passover? (30:3) (Ancient Practices, Time)

The Passover was usually celebrated on the 14th day of Abib, the first month of their calendar year. It is somewhere between mid-March and mid-April on our calendar.

318. How could Josiah overcome the negative influence of his ancestors? (34:2–3) (Family, Leaders)

Josiah was only eight years old when he became king, and he was probably raised by God-fearing people.

319. What did it mean to be stiff-necked? (36:13) (Meanings)

When Zedekiah was described as stiff-necked, it meant he stubbornly refused to turn to the Lord.

320. What were *Sabbath rests*? (36:21)
(Meanings, Sabbath)

Similar to how people are supposed to rest on the seventh day of the week, they were also to honor God by not farming their land and letting it rest every seventh year. (See Leviticus 25:4.)

Ezra

321. Why was family history so important? (2:59) (Ancient Practices, Family)

Being able to trace one's family history was important for establishing property rights and to show that a family had not been tainted by intermarriage after being in a foreign land.

322. Why couldn't those without family records serve as priests? (2:62) (Family, Priests)

⌐⇒ Men needed their family records to show that their ancestral line proved them worthy to be a priest.

323. Why did the Jews refuse the help of their enemies? (4:3) (Jewish Practices)

⌐⇒ The Jewish people were the only ones allowed to build the temple. Their help would taint the temple.

324. What did it mean that "the eye of their God was watching over" them? (5:5) (God's Power, Meanings)

⌐⇒ "The king's eyes" was the name given to Persian inspectors. The use of the word *eye* shows that God's knowledge and power is above that of the king's.

325. How long did it take to build the temple? (6:15) (The Temple, Time)

The project took about 22 years, from 538 to 516 BC.

326. What were the detestable practices of the neighboring peoples?

(9:1) (Idols, Unbelievers)

These practices represented a turning away from God that included worshiping pagan gods and may have included sacrifices and prostitution.

327. Why did Ezra confess guilt?

(9:6) (Guilt, Leaders)

As the leader of the community, Ezra identified himself with the community and offered a prayer of confession on behalf of all the people.

328. Is it wrong to marry someone of another race? (9:14) (Marriage)

No. In this passage Ezra was concerned about religious purity. Marriage to people from other nations often meant marriage to someone who doesn't believe in God.

329. How did God show his fierce anger? (10:14) (Anger)

The people were afraid that God was about to punish them, so they avoided his anger by changing their ways.

Nehemiah

330. What is a *cupbearer*? (1:11) (Ancient Practices, Food)

A *cupbearer* had to taste the food and drink before it was served to the king to be sure that it was not poisoned.

331. Why did some Jews sell their children into slavery? (5:5) (Ancient Practices, Slaves)

Sometimes ancient people who had little property would be forced to sell family members for a period of time in order to repay a loan.

332. How would intimidation lead to sin? (6:13) (Sin)

It would have been a sin to give in to Shemaiah's threats rather than trust in God.

333. Why was God described as swearing with an uplifted hand? (9:15) (Symbols, Vows)

God used this gesture to show that he vowed to keep his promise about the land. (See Exodus 6:8.)

334. What did it mean to "bind themselves with a curse and an oath"? (10:29) (Oaths, Punishment)

▭➔ The curse was meant to be a punishment if they failed to keep their promise to God.

335. What did it mean to cast lots? (10:34) (Ancient Practices, Meanings)

▭➔ This was a way to reach decisions like drawing marked sticks or pebbles. The Israelites believed God controlled the outcome.

Esther

336. Why was there a separate banquet for women? (1:9) (Food, Women)

▭➔ The king's banquet may have been considered too vulgar for women to attend because of all the drinking.

337. Why did no one check Esther's background before she became queen? (2:17) (Leaders, Women)

☞ The king and other officials may have thought it wasn't necessary because they were so impressed with Esther and her beauty.

338. Why did Mordecai disobey the king's command? (3:2–5) (Enemies, Truth)

☞ Mordecai knowingly disobeyed the command because he knew Haman was a wicked man who wanted to kill all of the Jews in the city. So Mordecai refused to honor him.

339. Why couldn't the king change his own laws? (8:8) (Pagan Practices)

☞ A royal law written in the king's name and sealed with his sign could not be stopped. That was a law.

340. How could someone who wasn't a Jew become a Jew? (8:17) (Jewish Practices)

To become a Jew meant to accept and obey Jewish laws like circumcision, observance of holy days, and dietary laws.

Job

341. Why does God allow his people to suffer? (1) (Suffering)

The simple answer is that we don't know why people suffer. Because we live in a fallen world, there is hardship and pain. But it is Satan who torments us, not God. Some suffering we bring on ourselves through bad choices or poor lifestyles. But often there is no clear explanation.

342. Was Job perfect? (1:1) (Perfection)

Job was not without sin, but he feared God and tried to follow God's law.

343. Was it wrong for Job to ask God why he was suffering? (10:2) (Suffering)

☐ No. Job wasn't being rebellious or challenging God's authority.

344. Why did Job ask God why he had been born? (10:18) (Sin)

☐ Job believed he could never satisfy the requirements of a righteous God and that God would always find some reason to punish him.

345. Is it wrong to be angry with God? (15) (Anger)

☐ It is natural to feel angry sometimes about life's hardships and even to blame God for allowing bad things to happen. Because we are made in God's image, God knows about our feelings and emotions, and he wants us to be honest with him. But at the same time, we need to be willing to accept God's will, even if it sometimes is difficult to understand.

346. How can I be a good comforter to my friends? (16:2–5) (Friendship)

Just like Job, most friends don't want to hear a long and critical speech if something has gone wrong. To be a good comforter, you should be encouraging and uplifting.

347. If God is all-powerful, why does he allow Satan to do evil things and to harm people? (19) (God's Power, Satan)

Although Satan's power has been destroyed for eternity, in our current world Satan still has some power. It is only when Christ returns that Satan's influence will no longer exist.

348. How did Job describe the injustice in the world? (24:2–12) (Suffering)

Job gave several examples of ways the poor and powerless were mistreated by others.

349. Did Job think God would judge the wicked? (24:22–24) (Judgment)

☞ Yes, but he wished that God would give righteous people the satisfaction of seeing it happen.

350. Is God beyond human understanding? (36:26) (God's Power)

☞ Yes. God is so magnificent that human beings cannot comprehend him.

351. Is God in charge of nature? (37:1–13) (God's Power, Nature)

☞ Yes. God displays his awesome power through nature.

352. What makes a person wise in heart? (37:24) (Wisdom)

☞ Those who are wise in heart believe that God never allows trouble to come to those who are righteous.

353. What can the animal kingdom teach us about God? (39:1–30) (Animals)

☐▶ The animal kingdom shows that God is pleased with variety. It also shows God's loving care for all creation.

354. Did God create dinosaurs? (40)
(Animals, God's Power)

☐▶ Yes. Although we don't know all the details about when dinosaurs lived or how they became extinct, it does seem clear that they were creatures that once inhabited the earth, and — like all other creatures — they were created by God.

355. In what way had Job's counselors not spoken what was right? (42:8)
(Fairness)

☐▶ They had claimed that wicked people always suffer and that righteous people always prosper, but that isn't always the case. Life isn't fair sometimes.

Psalms

356. What are some of the things the Psalms teach about? (Psalms)

☞ There are seven different kinds of Psalms that teach about thanking God, history, friendship, anger, confession, Jesus, and worship.

357. What does it mean to be blessed? (1:1) (Blessings, Meanings)

☞ It means to be filled with the joy that comes from serving God and having a strong relationship with him.

358. Why do many of the psalms ask God to punish wicked people? (5:10) (Psalms, Punishment)

☞ Instead of trying to seek revenge themselves, the writers of the psalms did the right thing by asking God to administer justice.

359. Did David have confidence in God?

(6:8–10) (Faith)

Yes. Even though he was sad, David was sure the Lord heard his prayer and believed his enemies would be punished as they deserved.

360. Does God sleep? (7:6) (God's Power)

No. God is not human and doesn't need sleep. By asking God to awake, David was just being impatient with God and wanted him to take action.

361. How is it possible for babies to praise God? (8:2) (Children, Worship)

Babies' cries and laughter give glory to God and please him. All of God's creation expresses praise to God, but it isn't always in the same way that we worship him.

362. How important are human beings?

(8:4–5) (Humans)

☞ Our importance lies in God. He honored human beings by putting them in charge of his creation.

363. May Christians question God? (13)

(Christians, Talking to God)

☞ Yes. God is willing to listen to us even when we are depressed or angry, and God is willing to allow us to ask him why bad things are happening to us. We can express these feelings to God but we shouldn't give up our faith that God will take care of us.

364. Was David really claiming to be sinless? (17:3–5) (Blame, Forgiveness, Perfection, Sin)

☞ No one is sinless, but God forgave David so he was blameless for his sins and tried to please God in everything he did.

365. Why does David call God his rock?
(18:2) (Faith, Meanings)

David had often taken refuge among the rocks in the desert. But he knew true security could only be found in the Lord.

366. Does being successful mean that God is blessing you? (18:37–42)
(Blessings, Success)

Everything good that happens comes from God, but lack of success does not mean that God is reserving his blessing.

367. How can I know God really exists?
(19) (Faith)

The existence of God cannot be proved. It is faith that allows us to believe in God, and faith is a gift of God through the Holy Spirit.

368. Did David need to be forgiven of sins he didn't even realize he had committed? (19:12–13) (Forgiveness, Sins)

Yes. People need forgiveness for all of their sins, but the sins that are committed deliberately are a form of rebellion against God. That is why David specifically asked God to keep him from willful sin.

369. Why did David say bulls, lions, and dogs were attacking him? (22:12–13, 16) (Meanings, Symbols)

The psalms often talk about attacks by wild animals to symbolize attacks by enemies.

370. Why is God compared to a shepherd? (23) (God's Love)

During ancient times, a shepherd was a metaphor that was widely used to describe kings in Israel and elsewhere in the Middle East. The Bible often refers to the Lord as the Shepherd of Israel to describe how deeply God loves his people.

371. Does God ever forget things? (25:6–7)
(God's Power)

God is not forgetful and always keeps his promises.

372. Why did David refuse to associate with sinful people? (26:4–5) (Sin)

David did not want to be influenced by their evil.

373. What does "wait for the LORD" mean? (27:14) (Meanings, Waiting)

This means trusting with patience and confidence that God hears and answers prayer even if they do not come immediately or the way we expect.

374. Why do the words "into your hands I commit my spirit" sound familiar? (31:5) (Jesus)

When Jesus was on the cross, he spoke these words right before he died. (See Luke 23:46.) Here, David was willing to trust his life or spirit to God.

375. Why is being silent such a bad thing? (32:3–5) (Forgiveness, Silence, Talking to God)

When we are silent, we are confessing our sins or asking for forgiveness from God.

376. David talks of taking refuge in a shadow. How can a shadow offer protection? (36:7) (Faith, Trust)

This was poetic language that showed David's desire for God to protect him as a bird protects its young.

377. What does it mean to be blameless?

(37:37) (Blame)

▶ Being blameless does not mean a person is without sin, but a person who continues to put his or her trust and confidence in God who grants forgiveness.

378. What will always happen to people, whether they are rich or poor? (49:5–9) (Death)

▶ Everyone will eventually die, and no amount of money can prevent death.

379. Did people in the Old Testament times believe in heaven? (49:15)

(Heaven)

▶ The Old Testament and the people in the Old Testament do not talk much about life after death because Jesus had not yet come.

380. What did God want more than sacrifices? (51:16–17) (Sacrifices)

☞ God takes delight in a person who has a humble heart and who turns to him to ask forgiveness.

381. What will happen to an evil person? (52:5) (Sin)

☞ God will bring him down, snatch him up, and uproot him.

382. Why was the olive tree so important? (52:8) (Meanings, Nature, Symbols)

☞ Ancient Hebrews believed the olive tree was a symbol of beauty, strength, prosperity, and blessing because the trees lived for hundreds of years.

383. Is it right to want our enemies dead? (55:15) (Enemies)

God teaches us to love our enemies; but in this case, David's enemies were also enemies of God.

384. Why did David lift up his hands?

(63:4) (Blessings, Symbols)

The Israelites lifted their hands in dependence on God, trusting that he would give them blessings.

385. What did it mean for God to ride on the clouds? (68:4) (God's Power, Meanings)

This was often used to describe the Canaanites' god, Baal. Instead, the author used that image to describe the power of God.

386. How was God a rock of refuge? (71:3)

(God's Power, Symbols)

A rock was a conventional symbol of security and safety. God was seen as a Protector of his people.

387. What was the author's hope?

(71:19–21) (Faith, Hope, Worship)

The author praised God even though he had experienced troubles because he believed God would restore him, increase his honor, and comfort him.

388. How can discipline be a blessing?

(94:12–13) (Blessings, Punishment)

Discipline is not just punishment, but directions and instructions in how to serve God, which leads people to happiness and peace.

389. How can we be joyful when things are not going our way? (100) (Faith, Joy)

When the Bible urges believers to be joyful, it does not mean that they necessarily forget their problems or their pain. What it does mean is that regardless of what happens in life, we understand that God is always in control, and his will controls the course of human events.

390. How are God's blessings transferred from one generation to the next?
(103:17–18) (Blessings, Family)

⬜➔ Those who love God train their children in righteousness and thus pass along the blessings.

391. Why do we say "Amen" at the end of prayers? (106:48) (Meanings, Prayer)

⬜➔ *Amen* means "It is true." Saying amen at the end of a prayer offers our approval for what was said.

392. How does God show concern for the poor? (113:7) (The Poor)

⬜➔ God cares for ordinary people and raises them up to greatness.

393. How would idolaters become like the idols they worshiped? (115:4–8)
(Idols, Worship)

☞ Those who worshiped idols would end up being helpless, powerless, and lifeless.

394. Why is death precious to God?
(116:15) (Death)

☞ The verse does not mean that God is glad when his people die, but he cares deeply and pays special attention because he loves those who follow him.

395. How can Christians meditate on God's Word? (Psalm 119) (God's Word)

☞ Meditation is a process of reflecting, reviewing, thinking, evaluating, feeling, and applying. We should read the Bible frequently and carefully, listening to what God is saying to us about our lives and our decisions.

396. Can people keep God's law perfectly? (119:1–3) (The Law, Perfection)

No. But those who love God try to live according to his commandments.

397. How can people hide God's Word in their hearts? (119:11) (God's Word)

Studying, memorizing, and reflecting on Scripture can help us understand how God wants us to live.

398. Do ancient laws still apply to people today? (119:52) (Ancient Practices, The Law)

Since God's law is based on his unchanging truth, it is still relevant for us today.

399. How does affliction serve as a positive influence? (119:67) (God's Word, Obedience, Suffering)

⬜ After experiencing suffering and abuse, we learn how important it is to obey God's Word.

400. Why is it bad to be double-minded? (119:113) (Sin)

⬜ Being double-minded means not making a commitment to one point of view or opinion, and God wants us to be fully committed to him.

401. Are we God's slaves? (123:2) (Slaves)

⬜ This is a comparison that emphasizes how people are humbly dependent on God and that he is a loving and kind Master.

402. Why didn't God keep a record of sins? (130:3–4) (Repentance, Sins)

▢⯈ God *does* keep a record, but he was quick to forgive people's sins if they repented and offered sacrifices.

403. Does God create each unborn child? (139) (God's Power, Life)

▢⯈ Yes. God is the Creator of life. Even though there are different methods of becoming pregnant or preventing pregnancy, God is the One who gives life, and his gift of life should be respected.

404. Why is it a kindness to discipline someone? (141:5) (Discipline)

▢⯈ If a righteous person corrects or disciplines someone so he or she will avoid evil, it would be a great kindness.

405. How can I know God's will for my life? (143) (God's Word, Prayer, Talking to God)

In Bible times God often spoke directly to people or sent messengers (such as angels) to communicate with people. Today, God has given us the Bible, which sets out general principles for believers, but it doesn't give advice for our specific situations. God wants us to pray about our questions, to discover answers through the Holy Spirit, and to seek advice from mature Christians who can often see our situation from a more objective perspective.

406. Why is remembering the past encouraging? (143:5-6) (God's Love)

Remembering the past often reminds you of times when God has taken care of you and will be encouraging for the present.

407. Does God provide everyone with what they need at all times? (145:14-16) (God's Love)

☐ The psalmist was painting a picture of God's marvelous goodness, but he was not saying that people never experience hardships.

408. Why should people not put trust in human beings? (146:3–4) (Humans, Trust)

☐ People should place their ultimate trust in God who is able to grant salvation.

409. Why doesn't God think it is important to be strong or fast?
(147:10–11) (Humans, Strength)

☐ God takes pleasure in his creation, but that pleasure isn't based on how strong or fast his creatures are. God takes pleasure in those who follow and serve him.

410. Who is called to praise the Lord?
(148:1–12) (Worship)

☐ All of creation is called to give praise to God because he is the awesome Creator of it all.

411. How should God be praised?
(150:3–6) (Worship)

God should be praised in a variety of ways with music and dance and expressions of thankfulness.

Proverbs

412. What does it mean to fear God? (1)
(Fear, Worship)

The word *fear* can also mean reverence or worship. Fearing God does not mean being afraid of God, but it may mean being careful to avoid offending or dishonoring him. Fearing God means obeying his laws and seeking to honor him with our behavior.

413. What is a *proverb*? (1:1) (God's Word)

Most *proverbs* are short, compact statements that express truths about human behavior.

414. What was the purpose of writing these proverbs? (1:2–7) (Wisdom)

The proverbs were meant to give a description of wisdom. Solomon wrote many of the proverbs and wanted to share his wisdom to give practical advice about living in a godly way.

415. How can wisdom save and protect people? (2:11–17) (Wisdom)

Having wisdom can save a person from giving in to the temptations offered by evil people.

416. Do righteous people always prosper and live long lives? (3) (Blessings)

No. As a general principle, God blesses those who serve him. But God's people can certainly experience suffering, and unrighteous people sometimes seem to thrive. Many Christians are poor, and many believers die young. God loves all of his people, and his promises about prosperity do not necessarily refer to material wealth, rather the feeling of peace and fulfillment that comes from obeying God's laws and the promise of everlasting life.

417. What is the ultimate source of wisdom? (3:19–20) (Wisdom)

God is the source of everything, including wisdom. Living by wisdom means to imitate the Lord and to conform to his plan for creation.

418. How should God's followers treat those who need help? (3:27–28)
(Generosity, The Poor)

▶ Throughout Scripture, God urges his people to care for those who are poor and needy.

419. Is wisdom the most important thing in life? (4:7) (Life, Wisdom)

▶ Yes. True wisdom begins with deep respect for God, which blossoms into a sense of sin and the need for salvation. Then wisdom leads people to seek God's will and to live godly lives.

420. Why is wisdom more valuable than silver, gold, or rubies? (8:10–11) (Material Possessions, Wisdom)

▶ Precious stones and metals cannot buy wisdom, godly character, or a close relationship with God.

421. Why is hard work praised? (10:4)
(Hard Work)

☞ Many proverbs criticize laziness as a cause of poverty and praise diligence and the rewards it brings.

422. Does God promise his people a life without trouble? (10:22) (Promises)

☞ No. Those who trust in God will be blessed by him but that doesn't mean they will have an easy life.

423. What is the day of wrath? (11:4)
(Judgment)

☞ This is the Day of Judgment when everyone will be called to account for what he or she has done.

424. Will a generous person always prosper? (11:25) (Blessings, Generosity)

☞ A generous person receives God's blessing, which is better than any earthly wealth.

425. When is it a good idea to remain quiet? (12:23) (Foolishness, Silence, Wisdom)

Wise people keep quiet so they don't share secrets or offer advice to people who won't take it. Foolish people speak without thinking of the consequences. Their words can be hurtful. Therefore, the wise know when to speak and when to remain silent.

426. Why are the friends you choose important? (12:26) (Friendship)

A righteous person chooses friends wisely, but a foolish person is often led down the wrong path by poorly chosen friends.

427. Why is it wrong to pretend to be rich or poor? (13:7) (Lying, Money)

Both of these are dishonest and deceptive. Both lead to folly.

428. Why is discipline so important?
(13:18) (Discipline)

☞ Discipline and correction are necessary to help keep a person on the path of wisdom.

429. Is joy only temporary? (14:13) (Joy)

☞ We should be prepared to deal with both joy and sorrow because while joyful times may not always end in grief, sometimes they do.

430. How do the righteous have a refuge even in death? (14:32) (Death, Faith)

☞ The faith of the righteous gives them hope beyond the grave.

431. What type of treasure do the righteous gain? (15:6) (Blessings, Material Possessions)

☞ This may refer to material wealth, but more importantly it speaks of the spiritual treasure of being blessed with godly character through doing God's will.

432. When are the poor better off than the rich? (15:16–17) (The Poor)

Love and peace within a poor family are far superior to riches when there is tension or anger.

433. What is the advantage of patience? (15:18) (Patience)

Impatience leads to impulsive words and actions that often lead to serious problems. Being patient is wise.

434. How were items weighed in ancient times? (16:11) (Ancient Practices)

Merchants carried stones of different sizes to balance the scales, which would weigh and measure quantities of silver for payment.

435. Why was gray hair a sign of honor? (16:31) (Age, Ancient Practices, Honor)

In ancient times, elderly people were treated with great respect.

436. Is it wrong to gossip, even if it's with my best friend? (16:38) (Gossip)

Gossiping about others can really hurt someone else's reputation. God wants us to look for the best in everyone and we aren't doing that even when we just listen to gossip.

437. Why is it important to hear both sides of an argument? (18:17) (Fairness)

Even if the person who first presents his or her case seems right, there is always another side.

438. How can helping the poor be a loan to God? (19:17) (The Poor)

Those who help the poor, for whom God has great love and concern, are in effect giving to God.

439. Why is making plans ultimately foolish? (19:21) (Foolishness, God's Power)

God will have the final word on how things turn out.

440. How are rich and poor people alike? (22:2) (Money)

Both must answer to God, their Creator.

441. Do my friends really influence my attitudes and behavior? (22:24–25) (Friendship)

A person's friends are the people they spend the most time around, which often means they are a large influence on that person's attitudes and behavior. This means we need to be very careful about the friends we choose.

442. How can we develop wise hearts? (23) (Wisdom)

Wisdom can come from loving God and honoring him by seeking to follow his will.

443. Is drinking alcohol bad? (23:20, 29–35)
(Drinking)

▭▶ The Bible warns adults about drinking too much because being drunk prevents a person from making good decisions. In the Bible it was acceptable for Israelites to drink alcohol and wine, but not to get drunk. God wants his followers to serve him and they can't do that if they are drunk.

444. Whom would wise people obey?
(24:21) (Obedience, Wisdom)

▭▶ They would obey the Lord and the Lord's representative, the king.

445. Why is it better for someone else to praise you? (27:2) (Boasting)

▭▶ Someone else will notice and offer praise if you deserve it, which is better than boastful comments you make about yourself.

446. How do people sharpen each other? (27:17) (Wisdom)

☐ Because people have different opinions and ideas, when they exchange those ideas or even argue about them, they both sharpen their ideas and their thinking and become wiser.

447. Why is hard work better than chasing fantasies? (28:19) (Hard Work)

☐ People who work hard will be sure to gain fruits from their labor.

448. Why is self-confidence foolish? (28:26) (Foolishness)

☐ Those who rely only on their own abilities and opinions are likely to be misguided, but those who seek wise counsel and try to follow God's commandments will be blessed.

449. What is the purpose of the rod of correction? (29:15) (Wisdom)

☐ This points to how discipline is seen as a way to help children gain wisdom.

450. What is the reward for godly character? (31:10–31) (Blessings)

⮕ A godly person can succeed in any aspect of life, including personal life in the home, professional life in a career, or as an individual in the community.

Ecclesiastes

451. Why was such a depressing book included in the Bible? (The Bible)

⮕ Ecclesiastes was written to show that no one can have a happy life without God.

452. How does God make life meaningful? (2:24–25) (God's Power, Life)

⮕ Life only has meaning and pleasure in God.

453. Can any person keep God's law perfectly? (7:20) (The Law, Perfection)

No one is able to perfectly obey God's law or to live a life without sin.

454. Why should people remember the times they suffered? (11:8) (Suffering)

This helps to keep things in perspective because people are not able to stay happy and well forever.

455. Why is it important to remember the Creator when we are young?
(12:1–5) (Young People)

Young people ought to remember God when their lives are still relatively free from pain, worries, and the infirmities and limitations of old age.

456. If life is meaningless, what should people do? (12:13–14) (Life)

Even if life is unpleasant and seems meaningless, it is important to fear God and serve him, and God will take care of the rest.

Song of Songs

457. Why is Song of Songs part of the Bible? (Marriage, Meanings, Sex)

This book was written for adults to help them understand that God created sexuality as a gift but also to serve as a warning to be sexually pure and experience sex only within marriage.

458. Why would a husband call his bride "my sister"? (4:9) (Ancient Practices, Meanings)

Lovers would often address each other as brother or sister in ancient times. They aren't actually brother and sister.

459. Why wasn't kissing in public allowed if they were married? (8:1) (Marriage)

In ancient times public affection was only allowed with immediate family members.

Isaiah

460. What are the last days? (2:2) (Judgment)

This could refer to the future in general or to a future time of judgment. The last days began with the coming of Christ and will be fulfilled when Christ comes again.

461. What are diviners and enchanters?
(3:2–3) (Meanings, Pagan Practices)

These are people who perform occult practices and snake charming. This was forbidden.

462. Why weren't young people and women considered to be leaders?
(3:12) (Leaders, Women, Young People)

In the ancient world, neither young people nor women were thought fit to be rulers.

463. What are *seraphim*? (6:2) (Angels, Meanings)

☞ *Seraphim* are angelic creatures. This Hebrew word means "burning ones," possibly referring to their purity.

464. Who is the child that is being referred to in this verse? (9:6–7) (Jesus)

☞ This points to the Messiah, a descendant of David.

465. What rights did the poor have? (10:2) (The Poor)

☞ The law gave the poor many rights. The weekly Sabbath, Sabbatical Year, and Year of Jubilee were designed to restore property to the poor and relieve their debts.

466. Why would God use a wicked nation to punish Israel? (10:5–6) (Israelites, Punishment)

God was totally in control and could use whatever means he wished to punish Israel, including using evil nations.

467. Why would God permit this violence toward women and children? (13:16)

(Suffering, Women, Young People)

This continues the imagery of God's wrath on the day of the Lord. In order to eliminate their evil influence, God sometimes allowed this type of cruelty toward the enemies of his people.

468. How certain were these prophecies?

(14:24–27) (Prophecies)

The Lord declared that his sovereign purposes would be carried out.

469. What was the Valley of Vision?

(22:1) (Biblical Places)

This was probably a valley near Jerusalem where God revealed himself to Isaiah in this vision.

470. Why would someone create his own grave? (22:16) (Ancient Practices)

The place of a person's burial was considered very important, and Shebna wanted to have a tomb that was as good as a king's.

471. Would the judgment effect everyone? (24:2) (Judgment)

There would be no distinction between people when the Lord came to deliver judgment; all would be judged.

472. Would God's punishment be universal? (24:6) (Punishment)

Because there was so much evil in the world, God's punishment would be widespread.

473. Does judgment teach righteousness? (26:9–10) (Judgment)

God can use judgment to get people's attention and prompt them to turn to him.

474. How would God judge the people?

(28:17) (Judgment)

⬛➤ The standards the Lord would use were his justice and righteousness.

475. Why were the leaders unable to understand the prophecies? (29:9–12)

(Leaders, Prophecies)

⬛➤ They had rebelled against the Lord for such a long time that they were unable to understand the meaning of his message.

476. Why was Jerusalem called Ariel?

(29:1–2) (Biblical Places, Names)

⬛➤ *Ariel* literally meant *altar hearth*. This may have been a nickname for the city because people came to worship at the temple altar in Jerusalem or it could also mean that fighting and bloodshed would turn the city into a place where many people would die as if sacrificed on an altar.

477. What should the people have done? (30:15) (Repentance)

The people should have repented and had confidence that God would protect them.

478. How does the Lord try to turn his people back to him? (30:20) (Hardship)

Sometimes God causes hardships to come to them.

479. What would happen when the Spirit was poured out on God's people? (32:15) (Blessings)

They would be blessed abundantly and live in peace.

480. What was the consuming fire? (33:14–16) (God's Presence)

This was the presence of the God of judgment.

481. What did it mean that God would allot their portions? (34:17) (Animals, God's Power)

God would give the desert creatures ownership of the land of Edom forever.

482. What are *cherubim*? (37:16) (Angels, Meanings)

Cherubim are winged creatures who existed to glorify God.

483. Why was grass growing on the roof? (37:27) (Nature)

Houses in this region were made of clay, and roofs were flat so the wind blew seeds onto the roofs, or they were dropped there by birds. But the soil wasn't deep enough for the plants to thrive, so they would wither and die.

484. Did the earth reverse its rotation?

(38:7–8) (Miracles)

God may have used a variety of methods to cause a shadow to go backward, but all of them would have been miracles to show his faithful servant that he would continue to live.

485. What was the good news? (40:9)

(God's Power)

This was not the same Good News that Christ brings, but the news that God would lead his people back to Judah.

486. What are the two images of God presented here? (40:10–11) (God's Love, God's Power)

God is presented as the powerful King or Ruler of all people but also as a gentle Shepherd who cares tenderly for his people.

487. In what way does this passage present a more tender image of God? (40:28–31) (God's Love, God's Power)

After Isaiah describes God's power and majesty, he stresses God's goodness to his people.

488. What were the ends of the earth? (41:5) (Biblical Places)

By 546 BC, Cyrus had fought his way to the west coast of Asia Minor. The ends of the earth were the boundaries of the lands he had conquered.

489. Who was the Redeemer? (41:14) (God's Power, Names)

The Lord is described as a kinsman-redeemer who would redeem his people's property, guarantee their freedom, avenge them against their enemies, and make their future safe.

490. When was God silent? (42:14)
(Waiting)

☐➔ God was silent when he allowed his people to be taken into captivity because he was waiting until the right time to bring judgment on Babylon and restore his people.

491. How was it possible for Israel to be taken captive? (42:24–25) (Punishment)

☐➔ The Lord was allowing his people to be punished for their disobedience.

492. What was significant about cedars, cypress, and oak? (44:14) (Nature, Symbols)

☐➔ These were the most valuable types of wood during this time period.

493. How great was the joy for the Lord's redemption of Israel? (44:23)
(God's Power)

All of nature was invited to give praise to God: the heavens, the earth, the mountains, and the forests.

494. Why would the Lord be called a God who hides himself? (45:15)
(God's Power)

This may be saying that the Lord's ways are mysterious to human beings and he is unlike the visible, man-made idols of surrounding nations.

495. How were the pagan gods limited in their power? (46:2) (Idols)

The pagan gods were taken into captivity along with those who worshiped them, unable to save themselves or their followers.

496. Why was the claim "I am, and there is none beside me" so wrong?
(47:8) (Lying)

☞ This was a truth only God had a right to claim for himself.

497. Why was Israel depicted as a barren woman? (49:21) (Symbols)

☞ Israel's barrenness, although a disgrace and tragedy, paved the way for God to adopt children from among the Gentiles.

498. How were these punishments a form of humiliation? (50:6) (Punishment)

☞ Beatings were for criminals or fools; pulling out the beard was a sign of disrespect and contempt; and mocking and spitting showed hatred.

499. What did it mean to drink the cup of the Lord's wrath? (51:17) (Judgment)

Experiencing God's judgment was often compared to becoming drunk on strong wine, making people stagger.

500. What did God's holy arm symbolize? (52:10) (Symbols)

God's arm often symbolized his power as well as the redemption and salvation he gave to his people.

501. What does the prophecy of the suffering servant foretell about the coming Messiah? (53) (Prophecies)

This extensive and well-known prophecy emphasizes that the Messiah would suffer greatly in order to pay the price for human sin.

502. How are people like sheep? (53:6) (Animals, Symbols)

Sheep are helpless and ignorant animals that often stray and get into dangerous situations.

503. What was an offering for sin? (53:10)
(Offerings, Sin)

▭➤ The person brought a ram to the priest for sacrifice, made amends for both unintentional and intentional sins, and paid a fine.

504. What covenant did God make?
(54:9–10) (God's Love, Promises)

▭➤ God promised his unfailing love to Israel.

505. How could hungry and thirsty people with no money buy wine, bread, and milk? (55:1) (Food, The Poor, Symbols)

▭➤ In the same way that God makes his gifts available to his people, the seller could make his goods available to poor buyers if he priced everything at zero.

506. What is the "everlasting covenant"? (55:3) (Promises)

The covenant with David was that his descendants would rule forever. Jesus, a descendant of David, fulfilled this promise and became the everlasting covenant.

507. How does creation praise God?
(55:12–13) (Creation, Worship)

Isaiah uses poetic language to emphasize that all of creation, including mountains and trees, will praise the Creator.

508. Where does God live? (57:15) (Heaven)

God, the high and lofty One, lives in a high and holy place—heaven. But he also lives within the hearts of the humble.

509. Why was their fasting not acceptable? (58:3–5) (Blessings)

☐➤ Their fasting was hypocritical because they did it in order to get God's blessing and were disappointed when he did not reward them. Their hearts and attitudes did not change and they continued to behave in ways that dishonored God.

510. What did God expect from his people? (58:6–9) (Generosity, The Poor)

☐➤ God expected that they would seek justice, free the captives, share with the poor, and provide clothing and safe haven for those without clothing or places to stay.

511. What were some of the sins of the people? (59:3–4) (Sin)

☐➤ They were guilty of violence, lying, injustice, and troublemaking.

512. Who would be drawn into the kingdom of God? (59:19) (Heaven)

☞ All nations from the east to the west would see God's saving work on behalf of his people and would honor him.

513. What does this image of light in the midst of darkness picture?
(60:1–3) (Symbols)

☞ Though the world seems to be covered in darkness, God's people reflect the light of God's love in their lives.

514. Why would their names be changed? (62:4) (Ancient Practices, Names)

☞ Changing names expressed a change in circumstances.

515. Did God make his people wander from him? (63:17) (Free Will)

God allowed his people the freedom to wander from him, but he certainly did not force them away from him.

516. What does it mean to wait for the Lord? (64:4) (Meanings, Waiting)

Waiting for God means to trust him and promise to serve him even when things are going badly. It means to have patient trust in God.

517. What does the image of the potter suggest? (64:8) (Symbols)

God is the artist, and we are his creation.

518. What were the new heavens and the new earth? (65:17) (Heaven)

This is talking about a time in the future when God grants his people salvation and everything will be transformed.

519. **What will life be like in the new kingdom?** (65:20–25) (Heaven)

⬛▸ People will enjoy long life, their work will be blessed by the Lord, the Lord will hear their prayers, and there will be peace in the land.

520. **Why were sacrifices criticized?** (66:3) (Sacrifices)

⬛▸ Sacrifices were only acceptable to God if they were offered sincerely and with a pure heart.

Jeremiah

521. **How did Jeremiah respond when God called him to be a prophet?** (1:6) (Prophets)

⬛▸ He claimed to be too young to be qualified to speak for the Lord.

522. How was Israel holy? (2:3) (Israelites)

Israel was set apart by God for a special purpose—to be the nation through which other nations would be blessed.

523. Why were the people drawn to worshiping idols? (2:8, 27) (Idols)

They may have believed that a different god lived inside each idol or they worshiped Assyrian gods to stay on good terms with the Assyrians.

524. What did it mean that they "had as many gods as they had towns"?

(2:28) (Idols, Meanings)

Every ancient town of any importance had its own patron deity, and many towns were named after their gods.

525. Why was Israel more righteous than Judah? (3:11) (Israelites)

Both Israel and Judah had rejected the Lord, but Judah's sin was worse because they chose to ignore Israel's example and the prophets God sent to preach to them.

526. Was God willing to accept his people if they returned to him? (3:22) (Blessings, Repentance)

Yes. God urged his people to repent and turn back to him, and he promised them blessings if they did.

527. What did it mean to "circumcise your hearts"? (4:4) (Sin, Symbols)

This was a way of saying that the people needed to cut the sinful behaviors from their lives.

528. What did God's challenge represent? (5:1) (Sin)

It was similar to Abraham bargaining with God to spare Sodom and Gomorrah. There were some righteous people in Jerusalem, but God was making the point that there were very few of them.

529. How were the people compared to unfaithful spouses? (5:7–8) (Idols)

Instead of keeping their vows to God, they turned away from him and committed "adultery" with other gods.

530. In what other ways did the people turn from God? (5:12–13) (Prophets)

They ignored the warnings of the prophets and didn't take them seriously.

531. How did the image of trapping birds paint a picture of the rich? (5:26–29) (Symbols)

It was comparing the way people would lure wild birds into a trap by placing tame birds inside a cage, with the way rich people set traps for the poor to snare even more wealth for themselves.

532. Is buying a lottery ticket or gambling wrong? (6:13) (Gambling)

While sometimes playing lottery games is fun, God doesn't want his followers to get too caught up in winning money. God knows that his rewards will last much longer than money.

533. What was the message of the false prophets? (6:14) (Prophets)

These false religious leaders ignored the sins of the people and promised a peaceful future even though God was about to punish them for their sins.

534. Why preach at the temple gate?
(7:1–2) (The Temple)

▭➤ Worshipers had to go through the gate to get to the activities in the temple court.

535. Why would bones be removed from graves?
(8:1) (Ancient Practices)

▭➤ Babylonians may have looted the graves to get the valuables that were buried with the kings and officials, which would have been a serious insult and sacrilege.

536. What wrong had the scribes committed?
(8:8) (Idols)

▭➤ They permitted the people to worship other gods in order to keep the peace, rather than insisting that they worship God alone.

537. How did God destroy Israel?
(9:16) (God's Power, Israelites)

▭➤ God scattered his people, so the nation was destroyed, but only for a generation.

538. How were idols made? (10:3–4) (Idols)

Idols were carved out of wood and then were plated with precious metals.

539. How many gods did the people worship? (11:13) (Idols)

The exact number isn't known, but their Canaanite neighbors had an estimated 2,000 to 3,000 gods.

540. Why had the Lord called his people an olive tree? (11:16) (Nature, Symbols)

An olive tree could live for hundreds of years, so it was a symbol of long life and productivity.

541. How was God always on the people's lips? (12:2) (Worship)

They spoke about God reverently, but they also worshiped other gods.

542. How would God restore his people?

(12:15) (God's Power)

▭➤ Eventually they would be brought back from exile to their own land.

543. What was the meaning of these questions? (13:23) (Meanings)

▭➤ These were rhetorical questions. The point was that the people had become so sinful that only God could change their ways.

544. Why would they cover their heads?

(14:3) (Clothing, Mourning)

▭➤ This was a common symbol of mourning.

545. Why did God seem like a stranger?

(14:8–9) (Idols)

▭➤ God seemed like a stranger to the people because they had separated themselves from him by following false gods.

546. What was God's glorious throne?
(14:21) (The Temple)

This was the temple in Jerusalem.

547. How would the people be winnowed? (15:7) (Judgment, Symbols)

Grain, after being harvested and threshed, was tossed in the air with a large winnowing fork, so that the wind would blow away the lighter straw and chaff and leave the grain behind. This is a picture of how God would judge the people.

548. Why did God tell Jeremiah not to get married? (16:1–4) (Marriage)

It may have been either to keep Jeremiah focused only on his ministry or because God wanted to spare Jeremiah from the pain the next generation would experience.

549. Why was their sin engraved with an iron tool? (17:1) (Sin, Symbols)

Iron tools were used to permanently chisel words in stone, which shows how pervasive their sin had become.

550. Why was Israel called a virgin? (18:13) (Israelites, Symbols)

This emphasized the people's earlier purity and commitment to God.

551. What did it mean to "inquire now of the LORD"? (21:2) (Meanings)

This meant to ask for knowledge or information, not necessarily to ask for help.

552. Why did God swear by himself? (22:5) (Oaths)

God did not need to take an oath because he always speaks the truth. But he did this for emphasis because there was nothing or no one greater to swear by.

553. What was the council of the Lord?
(23:18) (Leaders, Prophets)

This referred to those with whom the Lord shared his plans.

554. Is it possible for people to hide from God? (23:23–24) (God's Power)

Since God is everywhere, there is no place where people can hide and not be seen by him.

555. How is the true word of God described? (23:28–29) (God's Word)

It is described as grain (that can feed people), like fire (that can purify or destroy), and like a hammer (that can break something in its path).

556. How would the exiles return? (24:7)
(God's Power)

God would work in their hearts so they would return to him, and then they would be able to return to their land.

557. Why would grape treaders shout?

(25:30) (Ancient Practices, Food)

☞ People who were trampling grapes were usually in a happy mood because of the harvest, so they made lots of noise.

558. Who were the diviners, interpreters of dreams, mediums, and sorcerers?

(27:9) (Dreams, Pagan Practices)

☞ In the ancient Middle East, people placed great significance on dreams and their meaning. God told the people to ignore what the people who tried to interpret dreams said and to listen to his message instead.

559. Does God have a plan for each of us?

(29) (God's Power)

☞ Yes. We know that God loves his people and will care for us today as he has cared for his people in the past. We can try to discover God's plan for our lives by reading the Bible, praying, and seeking advice from parents and mentors.

560. Why would prophets sometimes be considered insane? (29:26) (Prophets)

Prophets often had very strange appearances and behaviors. The test for whether a person was a prophet or simply insane was whether or not their prophecies came true.

561. What were the days of old? (30:20) (Time)

This probably referred to the time when David was king and the kingdom was united.

562. When did people play timbrels? (31:4) (Ancient Practices)

Timbrels were usually played on joyful occasions, especially after a military victory.

563. Why were the exiles supposed to set up road signs as they left? (31:21) (Ancient Practices)

The signs would help them find their way back when they returned from exile. In the ancient world, road signs were tombstone-shaped markers.

564. What was the significance of the new covenant? (31:31–34) (Promises)

Because the people had broken the original covenant, God gave them a new one.

565. How did shepherds count their sheep? (33:12–13) (Ancient Practices, Animals)

Sheep were counted when they gathered around a watering hole, which made them much easier to count.

566. How would David be able to have an heir on the throne of Israel?

(33:17) (Leaders, Prophecies)

☞ This prophecy was fulfilled by Jesus, who was a descendant of David.

567. What was a funeral fire? (34:5) (Ancient Practices, Death, Leaders)

☞ This was not cremation but a memorial fire honoring the king who had died.

568. Why was it a curse for the dead bodies to be food for birds and animals? (34:20) (Ancient Practices, Animals, Death)

☞ It was a great dishonor in ancient times for a dead person not to be buried.

569. Why was there a special day of fasting? (36:6) (Ancient Practices)

A day of fasting was often proclaimed when there was a national emergency, in this case possibly the Babylonian attack.

570. Why did the men shave their beards, tear their clothes, and cut themselves? (41:5) (Clothing, Mourning)

These were all signs of mourning. They were probably mourning the destruction of Jerusalem.

571. Why did the women blame their husbands? (44:19) (Blame, Women)

The women said they weren't responsible for the idol worship because, in Jewish society, men could give their wives orders. So the men could have stopped them.

572. Why did conquering armies often spread salt on the earth of defeated territories? (48:9) (Ancient Practices, Battles)

They did this to make the land barren and unfit for farming.

573. Why did the Lord say the people would not be able to flee? (48:44) (Judgment)

The Lord's judgment was unavoidable.

574. Why would the marshes be set on fire? (51:32) (Battles)

The fires would be set to destroy the reeds so that fugitives could not hide there.

Lamentations

575. How was Jerusalem unclean? (1:8)
(Cleanness, Idols)

Jerusalem had become unclean because of her sin of idolatry.

576. Why would the people be searching for bread? (1:11) (Food)

Food shortages were a continuing problem during and after the siege of Jerusalem.

577. Why would God allow innocent children to suffer? (2) (Suffering, Young People)

God does not punish children with illness and starvation because of their disobedience or the disobedience of their parents. God's plan for his people is that they will be happy and will serve him, but that reality won't come about fully because no one is innocent of sin until the new heaven and the new earth.

578. How was God like an enemy? (2:4–5)
(Enemies, Punishment)

God had to punish Judah for its wickedness.

579. What comfort is given to people that God brings grief? (3:32) (God's Love)

Even though God judges sin and punishes wickedness, he is also a God of compassion and love.

580. Did the people resort to cannibalism? (4:9–10) (Battles)

During the siege of Jerusalem, some mothers actually cooked and ate their own children.

581. Why would people cry out, "Unclean!"? (4:15) (Cleanliness)

People who had skin diseases were required to call out, "Unclean!" when someone approached.

Ezekiel

582. Why did Ezekiel act in such unusual ways in order to communicate his prophecy? (3) (Prophecies)

☞ The prophets often were very unconventional in the way they ate, dressed, or behaved. Ezekiel's approach was designed to get the people's attention.

583. How would the people know the Lord had spoken? (5:12–13) (Punishment, Sin, Talking to God)

☞ God spoke through his actions saying that he would not allow their sin to go unpunished.

584. Why were the men's backs toward the temple? (8:16) (Idols, The Temple)

☞ Because almost all ancient temples faced east, these men who were worshiping the sun had their backs to the temple and to the Lord.

585. Why did the glory of the Lord depart? (10:18) (God's Presence, Idols, The Temple)

> The glory of the Lord left the temple because it had become defiled by the worship of other gods.

586. How did God take away their heart of stone and give them a heart of flesh? (11:19) (God's Power, Idols)

> God gave the exiles new hearts that were open to him rather than idols.

587. What were these detestable practices? (14:6) (Idols)

> These practices involved idolatry and pagan rituals including child sacrifice and animal worship.

588. **What was the new shoot the Lord would plant?** (17:22–24) (Nature, Symbols)

The Lord would take a shoot from David's family tree and use it to restore the dynasty of David.

589. **Does this verse provide a way to avoid physical death?** (18:21) (Death, Forgiveness, Repentance)

No, if a person repents and turns away from sin, God will forgive him.

590. **What was a *lament*?** (19:1) (Meanings, Mourning)

A *lament* was a chant usually composed for the funeral of a fallen leader. Here the lament is for the fallen nation of Israel.

591. Why was God concerned about his reputation? (20:9) (God's Power)

➡️ God wanted people to have a correct understanding of who he was and how he was in control of the history of his people.

592. How were Sabbaths a sign to God's people? (20:12) (Sabbath, Symbols)

➡️ Israel's observance of the Sabbath was to serve as a sign that they were God's holy people.

593. Who wore turbans? (21:26) (Clothing, Leaders, Priests)

➡️ Turbans, made of fine linen, were worn by priests or were worn as a setting for the crown for kings.

594. What type of prostitution was this? (23:5) (Politics, Symbols)

➡️ This refers to political alliances with pagan nations, not to idolatry.

595. What did the choice pieces of meat represent? (24:4) (Food, Symbols)

This referred to the people of Jerusalem who thought they had been spared from exile because of their goodness. (See Ezekiel 11:3.)

596. Did women in biblical times wear makeup? (23:40) (Women)

Women drew attention to their eyes by painting their eyelids with kohl, a soot-like compound used like eyeliner.

597. What was the point of the punishments of these nations? (25:7, 11, 14, 17) (Punishment)

God wanted people to recognize that he was the Lord and that he would not tolerate sin.

598. Why was the east wind so dangerous? (27:26) (Nature)

An east wind could be disastrous at sea and on land.

599. Why would they sprinkle dust on their heads and roll in ashes? (27:30)

(Ancient Practices, Mourning)

These were symbols of mourning.

600. What would life be like for the returning exiles? (28:26) (Life, Peace)

They would live in peace and safety in houses and vineyards — aspects of a good life.

601. What was the significance of forty years? (29:13) (Symbol, Time)

Forty years was sometimes used to symbolize a long and difficult period of time.

602. How did God explain that he was just? (33:17–20) (God's Power, Punishment, Repentance)

God said that he would punish those who turned away from him and spare those who repented and turned back to him.

603. How would God become the people's shepherd? (34:11–16) (Symbols)

The Lord would search for his scattered people and bring them back from captivity.

604. Why was the Lord so angry? (36:6) (Anger)

The Lord was offended by the ridicule of the nations because they were mocking and plundering his special land.

605. What were the new heart and the new spirit? (36:26) (Promises)

God promised that he would transform his people's minds and hearts.

606. What was a "land of unwalled villages"? (38:11) (Biblical Places)

This was a place of peace where walls or fortifications were not necessary.

607. How would the land be purified?

(39:14) (Ancient Practices)

After the seven-month burial period, special squads would be employed to ensure that the land was totally cleansed by making sure that any bones they found would be buried.

608. How would the people know that God was in charge? (39:21–23) (God's Power)

The people of Israel and the other nations would realize that the God who had saved and protected his people was now judging them for their sins.

609. What was the "Most Holy Place"?

(41:3–4) (Biblical Places, The Temple)

This inner sanctuary of the temple contained the ark of the covenant.

610. Why would the priests eat some of the sacrifices? (42:13) (Food, The Law, Priests, Sacrifices)

According to the laws God set forth in Leviticus, the priests were allowed to eat certain sacrifices.

611. Was the temple symmetrical?
(42:16–20) (Perfection, The Temple)

The temple was exactly as long as it was wide, which symbolized perfection.

612. What was the "glory of the LORD"?
(43:4–5) (God's Presence)

This was a physical display of God's presence and power among his people.

613. Why were the priests not supposed to perspire? (44:18) (Cleanliness, Priests)

Sweat would make the priests ceremonially unclean.

614. Why was contact with a dead person forbidden? (44:25) (Cleanliness)

Contact with a dead body made someone ceremonially unclean.

615. Why were the priests not supposed to own possessions? (44:28) (Material Possessions, Priests)

Because they had been set apart for special service to God, he wanted them to depend on him only.

616. What was the year of freedom? (46:17) (Ancient Practices)

This was the Year of Jubilee, held theoretically every 50th year.

617. How could foreigners become citizens of Israel? (47:22) (Jewish Practices)

God allowed foreigners to join with his people if the men agreed to the covenant of circumcision.

Daniel

618. Does God use dreams to speak to people today? (1) (Dreams, Talking to God)

Throughout the Bible there are many times that God spoke to people in dreams to show people what would happen in the future or to show people what they were supposed to do. However, God used dreams during ancient times because the Bible had not yet been written and now that we have God's Word in written form, it should be our guide for how to live.

619. Why would a captive be placed in a position of authority? (2:48) (Dreams, Leaders)

Daniel had proven he was able to interpret dreams and had dared to tell the king the truth.

620. What does the story of the blazing furnace teach about God? (3) (God's Power, Miracles)

God created this miracle to show that he was the only true God.

621. How confident were these men that they were doing the right thing? (3:17–18) (Trust)

They said that God could save them but that even if he didn't they would continue to place their trust in him.

622. What was a lions' den like? (6:7)
(Ancient Practices, Animals)

☞ It was a pit with a relatively small opening at the top, making it impossible for a prisoner to escape.

623. Why did Daniel face Jerusalem to pray? (6:10) (Ancient Practices, Prayer)

☞ It was customary for Jews who were away from Jerusalem to pray in the direction of the Holy City and God's temple.

624. Who was the Ancient of Days? (7:9)
(Names)

☞ This was a reference to God.

625. What did sackcloth and ashes symbolize? (9:3) (Mourning, Symbols)

☞ These were traditional signs of mourning.

626. What was the city that bore God's Name? (9:18) (Biblical Places)

▢➤ This was the city of Jerusalem.

627. How was the temple a fortress? (11:31) (The Temple)

▢➤ It was an earthly headquarters for the Lord, a source of strength for the Jewish people, and a central focus for their faith.

Hosea

628. Why did God tell Hosea to marry an adulteress? (1:2) (God's Love, Marriage)

▢➤ God was showing the people of Israel how God loved them even though they had behaved as an unfaithful spouse.

629. What would take the place of the bride-price? (2:19–20) (Ancient Practices, Marriage)

These five traits would make up the bride-price: righteousness, justice, love, compassion, and faithfulness.

630. Why would the people be "destroyed from lack of knowledge"? (4:6) (Punishment)

The people would be destroyed because they failed to know and to follow God's law.

631. Why didn't God want sacrifices? (6:6) (Repentance, Sacrifices)

Sacrifices had become empty religious rituals for many, and God wanted true repentance.

632. How could Israel reap the fruit of unfailing love? (10:12) (Blessings, Love, Repentance)

If Israel would repent and do what was right, she would be blessed by God.

633. How would God continue to love his people? (11:9) (God's Love)

God would punish the people of Israel but would not destroy them.

634. What did God promise? (13:14) (Promises)

God promised that even though he would punish them, he would restore them.

635. Why did they have to take words? (14:2) (Repentance, Sacrifices)

Sacrifices alone would not be enough. They had to express true repentance with their words.

Joel

636. How could a virgin grieve a husband? (1:8) (Ancient Practices, Marriage)

In Israel when a woman was promised to be married to a man, he was called her husband and she was called his wife, even before the marriage.

637. What did it mean that God was jealous for his land? (2:18) (Jealousy, Meanings)

God is described as jealous because he wanted his people to remain faithful only to him.

638. How could the locusts eat so much? (2:25) (Animals)

Each new wave of locusts ate what the previous wave had left behind.

Amos

639. How were Judah's sins different from the sins of the other nations?
(2:4) (The Law, Sin)

The other nations sinned against widely recognized laws of humanity, but Judah disobeyed the law given to them by God.

640. Why would a shepherd save part of the sheep? (3:12) (Ancient Practices, Animals)

This would prove to the owner that a wild animal had eaten the sheep and that it had not been stolen by the shepherd.

641. How had the Lord tried to turn his people back to him? (4:6–11) (Plagues)

The Lord had sent famine, drought, blight and mildew, locusts, plagues, and destruction to get the people's attention.

642. Why did the people need to prepare to meet their God? (4:12)
(Judgment)

☐▶ They were going to come face-to-face with God's judgment.

643. How did the people turn justice into bitterness? (5:7–13) (Justice)

☐▶ This section describes how the people had corrupted the process of justice in the courts with slander, bribery, and by intimidating witnesses.

644. What were ancient funeral processions like? (5:16) (Ancient Practices, Death, Mourning)

☐▶ Wailing relatives, often accompanied by paid mourners and musicians, walked ahead of the body that was being carried to the grave.

645. Why did Israel long for the day of the Lord? (5:18) (Blessings)

Israel expected to receive God's blessings when he came to judge the nations.

646. Why did God hate their religious festivals and offerings? (5:21–24)
(Justice, Offerings, Worship)

The people continued to observe the outward forms of worship, but they failed to promote justice and righteousness.

647. How did the people mistreat the poor? (8:6) (The Poor, Slaves)

They treated the poor unjustly and made slaves of them.

Obadiah

648. What can we learn about God from Obadiah? (God's Love, Promises)

Obadiah teaches about God's faithfulness to keep his promises.

Jonah

649. Was it really possible for Jonah to survive inside a huge fish for three days? (1) (Animals, Miracles)

Whales are mammals and have to surface occasionally to get air; it may have been possible for Jonah to survive in this way. But in any case, if a huge fish swallowed Jonah and spit him out after three days, it would have been a miracle.

650. How did someone receive "the word of the LORD"? (1:1) (God's Word, Prophets)

➥ This was a common phrase used to describe how a prophet received a divine revelation from God.

Micah

651. Why would the prophet go barefoot? (1:8) (Mourning, Prophets)

➥ Going barefoot was a sign of mourning.

652. How would God reward the traitors? (2:4) (Punishment)

➥ The traitors — the Assyrians — would take away the property of the rich, punishing them for abusing their poor neighbors, when they invaded the land.

653. Why would a lying prophet be right for these people? (2:11) (Lying, Prophet)

▭⟶ The people would be glad to reward someone for positive prophecies. They didn't want to hear the truth.

654. What did it mean to sit under one's own vine and fig tree? (4:4) (Peace, Symbols)

▭⟶ This was a picture of peace, security, and contentment.

655. What does God require from his people? (6:8) (Honor, The Law, Obedience, Worship)

▭⟶ God wants his people to live lives that honor him and that serve their fellow human beings. Believers respect God's laws and do their best to keep them as a form of thankfulness for their salvation. God did not want people to worship him with sacrifices unless they also loved him with their hearts and followed him with their lives.

656. How would nations react when they saw God's power at the Messiah's coming? (7:16) (God's Power)

⬚➤ They would be ashamed and frightened.

Nahum

657. Can people pass the point of being forgiven by God? (3) (Forgiveness)

⬚➤ It is only those who persistently reject God and defy him that will be cut off from his mercy. For God's children, however, nothing can separate them from God's love. God will forgive his people who are truly sorry for their sins and who wish to dedicate their lives to him.

Habakkuk

658. **Why were the Babylonians so greatly feared?** (1:8–9) (Fear)

☞ They attacked swiftly and they were cruel.

659. **Why did the prophet use this image of a net?** (1:15–16) (Symbols)

☞ The victims of Babylon were as helpless as fish caught in a net.

660. **Why was the grave called "greedy"?** (2:5) (Death)

☞ The grave never seems to be satisfied and always claims more people as everyone eventually dies.

Zephaniah

661. Why would people worship on roofs? (1:5) (Idols, Worship)

Incense was often burned to pagan gods on rooftops, and the kings of Judah had erected pagan altars on the roof of the palace in Jerusalem.

662. Why did the prophet urge the people to seek the Lord? (2:3) (Prophets)

Even though the destruction was about to take place, there was still time for the people to repent.

663. Is this book of prophecy meant to be a warning or an encouragement?

(3) (Prophecies)

Zephaniah is both a warning and an encouragement. Most of the prophecies balance the words of judgment with words of hope and restoration, telling how God will eventually save his people. These promises would help God's faithful followers get through the difficult times of judgment or punishment.

Haggai

664. What did the term *messenger* mean? (1:13) (Priests, Prophets)

This was another title for the prophets or priests of God.

Zechariah

665. Why was God angry with the people's forefathers? (1:2) (Anger)

☐ God was angry because they had broken the covenant, turned away from him, and disobeyed his laws.

666. What did it mean that Jerusalem would be a city without walls? (2:4–5) (God's Power)

☐ Walls would not be needed since God would keep them safe.

667. Where were the courts located? (8:16) (Ancient Practices)

☐ Legal matters were handled at the city gates.

668. Why were so many fasts observed?

(8:19) (Ancient Practices, Mourning)

The fasts were times of mourning. Since Israel had many experiences to mourn, several days of fasting were observed.

669. What does God want us to pray for? (10) (Prayer)

God wants us to talk with him about the big things and the little things of life. Zechariah wanted to teach the people to trust in God to provide everything that they would require. Acknowledging God as Provider by praying to him about everyday needs reinforces our faith in God's love and providence.

670. Why would the people need to be told that God controls the weather?

(10:1) (God's Power, Idols)

Many of the people worshiped pagan gods and thought the fertility god Baal controlled the weather.

671. Who is the shepherd? (13:7) (Names, Prophecies)

This was a prophecy about the Messiah, the Good Shepherd.

672. What is the Dead Sea like? (14:8) (Biblical Places)

The Dead Sea has the earth's lowest surface—1,300 feet (400 meters) below sea level. It measures about 47 by 10 miles (76 x 16 km). This sea is almost six times saltier than the ocean.

673. How would a drought affect Egypt? (14:18) (Food)

Rain was necessary to swell the Nile River so that it would flood its banks and deposit rich soil for crops.

Malachi

674. Why did God love Jacob and hate Esau? (1:2–3) (God's Love)

☞ God loved Jacob because of the covenant God made with him. He did not hate Esau but regarded him in a different way.

675. What type of animals could be sacrificed? (1:14) (Animals, Sacrifices, Vows)

☞ An animal sacrificed in fulfillment of a vow was supposed to be a male without defect or blemish.

676. What was the role of priests? (2:6–7) (Priests)

☞ In addition to offering sacrifices, priests were supposed to teach the law of Moses.

677. What was "the day of his coming"? (3:2) (God's Power)

☞ This referred to the day of the Lord, when God would complete his work in history.

New
Testament

Matthew

678. Why are there four different books in the Bible that tell about Jesus' life on earth? (1) (The Bible, Jesus)

The authors of these books were writing to different groups of people and had different purposes in mind when they were writing. Matthew wrote his book to prove to Jewish people that Jesus was the Messiah. Mark wrote his book for Gentile readers, possibly those who were facing persecution in Rome. Luke wrote to strengthen the faith of believers and to convince unbelievers that Jesus was the Savior for both Jews and Gentiles. John wrote his account of Jesus in order to convince his readers that Jesus was truly the Son of God. Together, they give us a description of Jesus that allows us to understand why he came to earth and to believe in him.

679. What did it mean to be "pledged to be married"? (1:18) (Ancient Practices, Marriage, Sex)

A man and woman could not have sex during their betrothal, but unlike a modern engagement it could only be broken by divorce.

680. What is "the kingdom of heaven"? (3:2) (Heaven)

It is a central part of Matthew's message and refers to God's rule in our hearts in the present reality and to his future kingdom here on earth.

681. Why would I want to get baptized? (3:5) (Baptism)

Baptism symbolizes someone's death to sin, burial of your old life, and resurrection in Christ. It should be done as a sign that someone accepts Jesus as Savior.

682. Why was Jesus tempted by the devil? (4:1) (Jesus, Satan)

Jesus' mission was to remain faithful to God and to conquer Satan.

683. In what three types of ministry did Jesus engage? (4:23) (Jesus)

The three main areas were teaching, preaching, and healing.

684. What does *beatitude* mean? (5:2–12) (Joy, Meanings)

The word means either "the joys of heaven" or "a declaration of blessedness, especially by Christ." It refers to the ultimate well-being and joy of those who share in the salvation of the kingdom of God.

685. What was Jesus' attitude toward the Law? (5:18) (Jesus, The Law)

Jesus did not come to get rid of the Law. However, he warned against trying to keep every commandment simply in order to win favor with God. Jesus taught righteousness comes through faith in Jesus and his work.

686. How did Jesus extend the meaning of the commandment against murder? (5:21–22) (Commandments, Meanings, Murder)

He said it also meant not having a hateful attitude toward another person.

687. What did Jesus teach about adultery? (5:27–30) (Jesus, Sin)

Jesus emphasized that a person's thoughts and intentions could be sinful even if his or her actions were not.

688. Is divorce always wrong? (5:31–32)
(Marriage)

Jesus was not creating a new law about marriage or divorce but was referring to the Old Testament law in Deuteronomy 24:1–4. Divorce is permissible in the case of unfaithfulness or adultery. But Jesus wanted to stress the value of marriage and criticized a casual attitude toward divorce.

689. Is hating someone a sin? (5:37) (Hate, Sin)

The Bible tells us to love and pray for our enemies. Even if someone has wronged you, God still wants you to be a light and forgive them like he forgives you.

690. How does the Lord's Prayer help us pray? (6) (Prayer)

Most Christians pray the Lord's Prayer because it is the prayer that Jesus taught his followers. The prayer gives Christians a model to follow when they pray to God.

691. Is praying out loud wrong? (6:5) (Prayer)

No. God wants you to pray to him however you like to, but he wants your prayers to come from your heart, not showing off how godly you can be.

692. Why isn't the ending to the Lord's Prayer included? (6:13) (Prayer)

Some manuscripts include it as a footnote; later manuscripts add "for yours is the kingdom and the power and the glory forever. Amen."

693. Is it wrong to worry? (6:25) (Worry)

No. But Jesus reminds us that worrying does not help us; instead, we should rely on God because he knows all our needs.

694. Did Jesus promise that we would get everything we pray for? (7:7–8)
(Prayer, Promises)

No. Jesus promised that the Holy Spirit will help guide us so that we will receive what we need, not necessarily what we want.

695. What did it mean to gnash one's teeth? (8:12) (Anger, Meanings)

In the Old Testament, this expression represented rage, anger, or hatred. In the New Testament, the phrase represented disappointment or agony of spirit.

696. Who were the Samaritans? (10:5)
(Enemies, Israelites)

The Samaritans were a race of people that came from the intermarriage of Israelites left behind when the people of the northern kingdom were exiles, and Gentiles who were brought into the land by the Assyrians. There was a bitter hostility between them and the Jews.

697. Who was Beelzebub? (10:25) (Satan)

⬜▶ This name refers to Satan.

698. Why didn't Jesus want people to tell others who he was? (12:16) (Jesus)

⬜▶ There may have been several reasons: he did not want to be thought of as just a miracle worker; he may not have wanted his teaching ministry to be overshadowed by the healing miracles; he didn't want the authorities to arrest him before his ministry was accomplished; or possibly he didn't want the crowds to grow even larger and make it more difficult for him and the disciples to move from place to place.

699. What was the unpardonable sin? (12:31) (Sin)

⬜▶ The context suggests that the sin that would not be forgiven was claiming that Jesus' miracles done in the power of the Holy Spirit were really caused by Satan.

700. Why did Jesus use parables? (13)

(Jesus, Parables)

Jesus used parables because people could easily remember the stories that he used because they were from everyday life. He also used parables because some of the ideas that he was trying to get across to his followers were not always easy to understand. Jesus' parables give a hint of an important truth about God and his kingdom, but they do not tell the whole story.

701. What is a mustard seed really like?

(13:32) (Meanings, Parables)

The mustard seed is not really the smallest seed known today, but it was the smallest seed that farmers in the Holy Land used. Under the best conditions, a mustard seed can produce a plant that can be up to ten feet tall.

702. Why did Jesus have to pray? (14:23)
(Prayer, Talking to God)

Jesus used prayer as a way to communicate with God the Father and the Holy Spirit. He asked God for help and guidance and thanked him for his love — the same way we pray.

703. What were the "gates of Hades"?
(16:18) (Biblical Places, Death)

The gates of Hades may mean the powers of death or the forces that oppose Christ and his kingdom.

704. What were the "keys of the kingdom"? (16:19) (God's Power, Symbols)

These were symbolic keys that represented power and authority given from God.

705. What did Jesus teach about forgiveness? (18) (Forgiveness, Jesus)

Throughout history God has shown mercy to his people and has forgiven them when they have turned to him after they sinned. God expects his people to extend the same kind of love and forgiveness to other people. Christians should not keep count of the times that they forgive others, but should continue to forgive because they have been forgiven in an even greater way by God.

706. What did it mean that Jesus was transfigured? (17:2) (God's Power, Jesus, Meanings)

Transfigured means that Jesus' appearance was changed. His disciples saw him as he would appear in heaven.

707. Did Jesus really want us to act like children? (18:3–4) (Children, Jesus)

Jesus wanted his followers to be humble like a child that still depends on and trusts his parents to provide everything he needs. Jesus wants us to depend and trust him that way.

708. Do we have guardian angels? (18:10)
(Angels)

▭ Jesus was emphasizing here that every person is important to God. Even children are important enough to be looked after by angels.

709. Do believers need to sell everything they own to get to heaven? (19:21)
(Heaven, Material Possessions)

▭ No. Jesus was saying that his followers need to give up whatever they love more than him.

710. Did they believe it was possible for a camel to fit through the eye of a needle? (19:24) (God's Word, Jesus, Symbols)

▭ Jesus was using exaggeration to help his disciples understand that people's love of money and things can hurt their spiritual life.

711. What did Jesus mean by "the first will be last"? (19:30) (Heaven, Jesus, Meanings)

The things that matter are the things that seem weak or less valuable to the rest of the world but will be first in God's kingdom.

712. Who was the Son of Man, and how would he be "delivered over"?
(20:18–19) (Jesus)

Jesus was the Son of Man, and here he was predicting his betrayal by Judas, as well as his death and resurrection.

713. What did *Hosanna* mean? (21:9)
(Meanings)

The word originally meant "save now, pray," but by New Testament times it had lost its primary meaning and had become an exclamation of praise.

714. What are phylacteries? (23:5) (Jewish Practices, Meanings)

Phylacteries are little boxes strapped to the arm or forehead that contain strips of paper on which Scripture passages are written. There were four specific verses: Exodus 13:1–10; 13:11–16; Deuteronomy 6:4–9; and 11:13–21.

715. Where exactly is the Mount of Olives? (24:3) (Biblical Places, Jesus)

The Mount of Olives is a ridge a little more than a mile beyond the Kidron Valley east of Jerusalem.

716. Will the arrival of the Messiah be a secret? (24:27–28) (Jesus)

Jesus said that his second coming would be as obvious as lightning or the circling of vultures.

717. How are people rewarded for what they do to serve others? (25:34–40)

(Blessings, Heaven)

Rewards in the kingdom of heaven are given by grace to those who serve without thought of a reward.

718. What exactly was Barabbas' crime that he was to be crucified? (27:16)

(Death, Jesus, Punishment)

Barabbas had taken part in a rebellion, probably against the Romans. He may have been a sort of folk hero to the Jews. Matthew calls him a notorious prisoner, but the other Gospel writers say he may have been arrested for robbery, sedition, and murder.

719. How severe was the punishment of flogging? (27:26) (Punishment)

Roman floggings were so harsh that sometimes the victim died before being crucified.

720. When did the earthquake take place? (28:2–4) (Time)

☐➤ It is clear from the accounts in Mark, Luke, and John that the earthquake had taken place before the women arrived at the tomb.

721. Why were there only eleven disciples? (28:16) (Disciples)

☐➤ Judas had committed suicide (27:5).

Mark

722. Why would John the Baptist have eaten such unusual foods? (1:6) (Food, Jewish Practices)

☐➤ No one who lived in the desert at this time would hesitate to eat insects, and locust were part of the ceremonial foods that Jews could eat. John's simple diet and lifestyle showed his focus on his work for God.

723. How was the Trinity revealed at Jesus' baptism? (1:10–11) (Baptism, Jesus, Trinity)

All three persons of the Trinity were involved: the Father spoke, the Son was baptized, and the Spirit descended like a dove.

724. Why did the demon call Jesus the "Holy One of God"? (1:24) (Evil Spirits, Jesus, Names)

The name may have been used by the demons out of fear or out of an attempt to exercise control over him.

725. What did the Jewish people think about tax collectors? (2:14) (Jewish Practices)

Because tax collectors were Jews who collected tolls for Rome, they were considered traitors. They also were considered extremely dishonest. They could not serve as witnesses or judges, and they were expelled from the synagogue.

726. What did Jesus mean when he said, "the Sabbath was made for man"? (2:27) (Jesus, Sabbath)

Jewish traditions had built up so many requirements for the Sabbath that the burden had become enormous, but it was meant to be a day of spiritual, mental, and physical restoration.

727. Why did Jesus say that parables would keep some people from understanding? (4:11–12) (Jesus, Parables)

Jesus compared his preaching to the ministry of Isaiah who gained some followers but who also exposed the resistance of many people to God's warnings and calls for repentance. Those who desired to hear would understand, but those who were rebellious would not.

728. Why didn't the disciples know who Jesus was? (4:41) (Disciples, Jesus)

When they saw Jesus miraculously calm the storm, they were amazed and asked rhetorically who Jesus was as a statement of awe.

729. What type of illness did the woman have? (5:25) (Sickness)

The exact nature of her problem is not known, but her life would have been miserable because she was shunned by people for being ceremonially unclean.

730. Why did Jesus tell people not to spread the word about his miracles? (5:43) (Jesus, Miracles)

His popularity — along with the opposition from the religious leaders — could have created a crisis before he was finished with his ministry.

731. Was Jesus a carpenter? (6:3) (Jesus)

Matthew reports that Jesus was a carpenter's son. The question in this verse was a negative one, implying that Jesus was just a common laborer.

732. What did it mean that the disciples' hearts were hardened?
(6:52) (Disciples)

They hadn't understood the significance of the miracle of feeding the 5,000. The miracle showed that Jesus was the Son of God.

733. Why did Jesus criticize the Pharisees and teachers of the law?
(7:6–8) (Jesus, Pharisees)

Jesus called them hypocrites for following the traditions of washing their hands but not loving God with their hearts.

734. What was Jesus' radical message?

(7:19–20) (Cleanliness, Jesus)

Mark points out that Jesus said uncleanness came from an impure heart, not from eating certain foods. In effect, Jesus declared all foods clean.

735. Why did Jesus avoid the term *the Messiah?* (8:29) (Jesus, Names, Politics)

Jewish people associated the term *Messiah* with political and national ideals, so Jesus generally avoided using the term to describe himself.

736. Why were the disciples not to tell people what they'd seen until after the resurrection? (9:9) (Disciples, Jesus)

Jesus wanted the disciples to be able to communicate his finished or completed work, which would demonstrate his full identity as the Messiah.

737. What are demons? (9) (Evil Spirits)

Demons are evil spiritual beings that are opposed to God and human beings. In the Bible demons have various powers. They could take over a person and control a person's speech and actions. They often caused people to become physically and mentally ill.

738. Why would Jesus' friends argue about who was the greatest? (9:34)

(Jesus, Power)

Questions and concerns about rank and status were very important to Jewish people at this time. These men were no different than the rest of the people at that time. But Jesus did not place any importance on rank or status.

739. What did Jesus really mean when he talked about cutting off a hand or a foot? (9:43) (Jesus' Teaching)

This was an exaggeration. What Jesus was really saying here is that anything that got in the way of God's kingdom should be eliminated.

740. What did Jesus mean that the kingdom of God belonged to children? (10:14) (Children, Jesus)

The kingdom of God belongs to those who, like children, can receive it as a gift.

741. What was Jesus' role? (10:45) (Jesus)

Jesus came to earth as a servant who would suffer and die to redeem people from their bondage to sin and death.

742. What did Jesus mean when he asked if John's authority was from heaven or of human origin? (11:30)

(Heaven, Jesus, Names)

☞ *Heaven* was a common Jewish term for God, and it was often substituted for his name to avoid misusing it.

743. What do the bread and the wine represent? (14:22–24) (Food, Symbols)

☞ Jesus gave a new meaning to the Passover celebration by saying that the bread represented his body and the wine represented his blood.

744. Where did the term *Eucharist* come from? (14:23) (Meanings)

☞ The term *Eucharist*, another name for Communion or the Lord's Supper, came from the Greek word translated as "giving thanks".

745. What does *Abba* mean? (14:36)
(Meanings)

This is an Aramaic word that was a small child's way of saying "Daddy."

746. Why was Jesus, of all people, accused of blasphemy? (14:64) (Jesus, Punishment)

Blasphemy included insults to God or any challenge to his authority or majesty. Since Jesus claimed to be the Messiah, the Son of God, some people considered that blasphemy.

747. Why did Jesus have to suffer and die? (15) (Death, Jesus, Suffering)

Because God is merciful, he sent his Son down from heaven to redeem the world from the sin and consequences of pain and death brought on by Adam and Eve. By paying the price for sin, Jesus set believers free from eternal punishment and gained for his people God's grace, righteousness, and eternal life.

748. What did it mean to be crucified?

(15:24) (Ancient Practices, Meanings)

This was a Roman means of execution in which a victim was nailed to a cross. Heavy nails were driven through the wrists and heel bones. Then the cross was raised. As the victim hung there, it was difficult to breathe. At a certain point, if the person was still alive, his legs were broken to hasten death by suffocation. Only slaves, the worst criminals, and people who weren't Roman citizens were executed in this way.

Luke

749. Why is Mary's song known as the Magnificat? (1:46–55) (Meanings)

In the Latin translation of the Bible, the first word of her song is *magnificat*, which means "glorifies."

750. Did Jesus really live on the earth?
(2) (Jesus)

Yes. Even though Jesus is God, he took on human form and became a living human being. Jesus was a living human being in every way, except for the fact that he was without sin. Because Jesus lived on earth as a human being, he understands our human situation, our pains, and our hurts.

751. What was the town of David? (2:11)
(Biblical Places)

The town of David was actually Bethlehem.

752. What is a *manger*? (2:7) (Animals, Meanings)

This was a feeding trough for animals.

753. What did Jewish boys begin to do at age 12? (2:42) (Jewish Practices, Young People)

At age 12, boys began preparing to take their places in the religious community the next year.

754. Where did the temptation of Jesus take place? (4:1–12) (Biblical Places, Jesus, Temptation)

The temptations of Jesus took place in a wilderness region in the lower Jordan Valley, on a high mountain, possibly near Jericho and on the highest point of the temple where the priests went to blow a trumpet to announce important events.

755. Who were the Pharisees and teachers of the law? (5:17) (The Law, Pharisees)

The Pharisees were a legalistic and separatist group who strictly obeyed the laws of Moses and the other traditional laws of the elders that had been passed down. The teachers of the law were scribes who studied, interpreted, and taught the law.

756. What was the heart of Jesus' teaching? (6:27) (Jesus, Love)

The heart of Jesus' teaching was love — even love for one's enemies.

757. Who were the elders of the Jews? (7:3) (Jewish Practices, Leaders)

These were respected leaders in the community.

758. What were the "secrets of the kingdom of God"? (8:10) (Truth)

These were truths that could only be known if God revealed them.

759. Why were the disciples not supposed to take anything with them? (9:3) (Disciples, Material Possessions)

They were supposed to depend on the hospitality of the townspeople and what God provided them with.

760. What did Jesus require from his followers? (9:23) (Disciples, Jesus, Obedience)

Jesus said that those who followed him would have to deny themselves and obediently follow him.

761. Why did Moses and Elijah appear? (9:30–31) (God's Power, Prophets)

Together they represented the way God had led his people throughout their history.

762. Who were the Samaritans? (10:33) (Meanings)

This was a race of people resulting from the intermarriage of Israelites who were left behind when the people of the northern kingdom were exiled and Gentiles who were brought into the land by the Assyrians.

763. What was the value of two denarii? (10:35) (Money)

☐➔ This would be equal to about two days' wages and would be enough to pay for about two months' lodging in an inn.

764. What did it mean to forgive sins?
(11:4) (Forgiveness)

☐➔ Jesus speaks of daily forgiveness as being necessary to restore communion with God.

765. What did Jesus mean about putting a light where it could be seen?
(11:33) (Symbols)

☐➔ He wants people to be like him and publicly exhibit the light of the gospel.

766. Are small sins treated the same way as big sins?
(12:10) (Sin)

☐➔ In God's eyes all sins are equal. God wants you to be faithful in both large matters and small matters.

767. What does it mean to seek God's kingdom? (12:31) (Heaven)

➡️ Jesus meant that his disciples should seek the spiritual benefits of God's kingdom rather than material things.

768. Who will be included in the kingdom of God? (13:29) (Heaven)

➡️ Believers from all across the world and from among all people will be part of God's kingdom.

769. Did Jesus really mean that his followers had to hate their parents and other family members? (14:26) (Family)

➡️ Certainly not. This was an example of exaggeration that Jesus used to show that a believer had to love Jesus even more than his or her family.

770. What kind of coin was this parable referring to? (15:8) (Ancient Practices, Meanings)

The silver coins were probably drachmas. A drachma was a Greek coin that was approximately equivalent to a Roman denarius, worth about a day's wage.

771. What is hell like? (16) (Hell)

Hell is the place of eternal punishment for those who have rejected God. All human beings who are God's children will live with him in heaven forever, and those who are not his children will suffer in hell forever. When the Bible speaks of hell, it often refers to it as a place of fire. We do not know if the fire is literal or if it is a symbol for the pain that people suffer when they are separated from God for all of eternity.

772. Is it wrong to cheat on a test? (16:10)
(Lying, Sin)

Cheating is lying to your teacher, saying that you did all your own work when you didn't. God tells us that lying is a sin, which makes cheating a sin too.

773. Should we limit the number of times we forgive others? (17:4)
(Forgiveness)

No. Jesus used the number seven — which symbolized perfection — to emphasize the importance of forgiveness.

774. What will happen at the final judgment? (17:35) (Judgment)

People will be taken to destruction or taken into the kingdom.

775. Why did the blind man call Jesus the "Son of David"? (18:38–39) (Jesus, Names)

This was the title of the Messiah and acknowledged that Jesus was the heir of David's throne.

776. Why would Jesus ride on a donkey? (19:30) (Animals, Jesus, Symbols)

A king rode on a donkey. Jesus did this to show that he was the chosen Son to sit on David's throne.

777. What will happen to those who reject Jesus? (20:17–18) (Jesus)

They will be like a pot that is smashed against a stone or like someone who has a stone fall on him or her and is crushed.

778. What were synagogues used for?

(21:12) (Jewish Practices)

They were used not only for worship and school, but also for community administration and confinement while awaiting trial.

779. Why did Jesus want to celebrate this Passover with his disciples?

(22:14–16) (Disciples, Food, Jesus, Jewish Practices)

This would be the last time Jesus could share a meal with them before he himself became the "Passover Lamb" and sacrificed his life to redeem the world.

780. What did Jesus say about his disciples' desire for greatness?

(22:25–27) (Disciples, Jesus)

People should not seek greatness in the kingdom of God but instead should achieve great things by being willing to serve others, just as Jesus did.

781. Did Jesus really die and come back to life? (23–24) (Death, Jesus, Life)

Yes. Just as Jesus truly was born, he truly died. He hung on the cross for several hours, and many witnesses were there to observe it. By dying, Jesus became the sacrifice for the sins of the world. Jesus also rose from the dead. Jesus arose and by rising from the dead, Jesus overcame death and guaranteed that believers would also overcome death and live with him forever.

782. Why did Simon have to carry the cross? (23:26) (Ancient Practices)

Men who were to be crucified were usually forced to carry a beam of their cross weighing 30 to 40 pounds (14 to 18 kg) to the place of crucifixion. Jesus began by carrying the cross, but he was not able to carry it the whole way.

783. How were bodies prepared for burial? (23:55–56) (Ancient Practices, Death)

Yards of cloth and large quantities of spices were used in preparing a body for burial.

784. Were tombs usually sealed with stones? (24:2) (Ancient Practices, Death)

A tomb's entrance was normally closed to keep vandals and animals from disturbing the bodies. This stone had been sealed by the Roman authorities because they didn't want Jesus' disciples to take the body and claim that he had risen from the dead.

John

785. Who created God, and where does he live? (1) (God's Power, Heaven, Time)

God is beyond the human idea of time. He has always existed and will always exist; he is eternal. And he is a spirit rather than a physical being. He is present everywhere.

786. Why are light and life important images for this book? (1:4) (Life, Symbols)

John linked Christ with the image of light, particularly the "light of the world," who offers eternal life to humankind.

787. Why was Jesus called the "Lamb of God"? (1:29) (Animals, Jesus, Names)

The term refers to Jesus as the sacrificial Lamb who would atone for the sins of the world through his death.

788. Why is John 3:16 so important? (3:16) (Meanings, Promises, Salvation)

John 3:16 promises Christians that all we have to do is believe in Jesus to be saved.

789. Why would the disciples have been surprised that Jesus was speaking with a woman? (4:27) (Disciples, Jesus, Jewish Practices)

They were surprised probably because Jewish religious leaders rarely spoke with women in public, and Jews typically did not associate with Samaritans at all.

790. What did it mean that Jesus was the Savior of the world? (4:42) (Jesus, Salvation)

This pointed to the fact that Jesus' salvation extended to the entire world, to all who believed.

791. Why did the Jews want to kill Jesus? (5:18) (Jesus, Murder)

They considered Jesus' claim — that he had a special relationship to the Father that made him equal to God — as blasphemous.

792. What did Jesus call himself in the book of John? (6:35) (Jesus, Names)

Jesus said he was the bread of life (6:35); the light of the world (8:12); the gate for the sheep (10:7); the good shepherd (10:11, 14); the resurrection and the life (11:25); the way, the truth, and the life (14:6); and the true vine (15:1).

793. Is Jesus eternal? (8:58) (Jesus, Life)

Yes. When he said "I am," he echoed God's words in Exodus 3:14. This expressed Jesus' eternal existence and his oneness with the Father.

794. Why did the disciples ask who had sinned? (9:2) (Disciples, Sickness, Sin)

The rabbis taught that if someone suffered from a physical ailment, then the person or his parents or grandparents had sinned. They even believed that a person could sin before birth.

795. Why did Jesus refer to himself as the shepherd? (10:11–18) (Jesus, Leaders, Names)

In the ancient Middle East, the ruler was considered a shepherd to his people. Jesus is the Good Shepherd who died to make a way for his sheep to be with him forever.

796. Why was the fact that Lazarus had been dead for four days so final? (11:17) (Death)

Many Jews believed that the soul remained near the body for three days after death in hope of returning to it.

797. Who had the power to stop Jesus? (11:47) (God's Power, Jesus)

The Pharisees seemed to be Jesus' principal opponents during his ministry, but it was the chief priests who were prominent in the events leading to his crucifixion. Ultimately, no one could stop

Jesus. It was Jesus' plan from the beginning to die for our sins.

798. How did the voice from heaven confirm what Jesus was about to do? (12:28–33) (Jesus, Sacrifice)

The voice from heaven affirmed that the Father had been glorified by Jesus' willingness to make himself a sacrifice.

799. Why did Jesus wash his disciples' feet? (13:5) (Ancient Practices, Jesus)

Etiquette demanded that a host make sure that his guests' feet were washed generally by the lowest servant in the household. Jesus wanted to teach his disciples a lesson about servant-hood.

800. Why did Peter tell Jesus not to wash his feet? (13:8) (Ancient Practices, Jesus)

He misunderstood Jesus' actions. Peter may have felt humbled by the prospect, while at the same time feeling that Jesus was demeaning himself.

801. Why was eating bread together an important activity? (13:18) (Food, Symbols)

It was a sign of close friendship.

802. Why was Jesus troubled? (13:21) (Jesus)

Even though Jesus knew what was about to happen, he was grieved by the fact that Judas would betray him.

803. Is Jesus really the only path to salvation? (14) (Jesus, Salvation)

When Jesus said he was the only way to God, he was making an exclusive claim. He said that faith in him was necessary for salvation.

804. Is Jesus the only way to God? (14:6)
(Jesus)

Only through belief in Jesus as our Savior are we assured a place in heaven with the Father.

805. Why was the Holy Spirit referred to as an advocate? (14:16) (Holy Spirit, Sin)

The term refers to the Holy Spirit's role as the one who convicts us of sin but who is also our guide and comforter.

806. Does obedience or love come first?
(14:21, 23) (Love, Obedience)

Neither. Love and obedience complement each another. Loving God and obeying him are part of a single act.

807. How can God be three Persons in one? (15) (Trinity)

God is beyond human understanding, so we cannot explain in human terms exactly how there can be one God with three Persons. The Father, the Son, and the Holy Spirit are each fully God, but also distinct.

808. Why did Jesus say that he chose his disciples? (15:16) (Disciples, Jesus)

Normally disciples chose the rabbi they would follow, but Jesus had chosen his disciples with the purpose of having them bear fruit.

809. Why did the people Jesus spoke to have no excuse for not believing in him? (15:22) (Faith, Jesus)

He had appeared to the Jewish people directly, and they had the benefit of having access to God's words in the Old Testament.

810. Why would the Holy Spirit not come until Jesus had gone away?

(16:7) (Holy Spirit, Jesus)

We had no need of the Spirit while Jesus was on the earth.

811. Why did Jesus ask to be glorified?

(17:5) (God's Power, Jesus)

Jesus asked the Father to return him to his previous position of glory to show that he had fulfilled the work he set out to do — demonstrating God's love and power.

812. If God wants his followers to be as one, why are there so many types of Christianity? (17:20–23) (Christians)

Different types of Christianity have come from people emphasizing different things in the Bible. God does want us to be unified, but true unity can only come from God himself.

813. Why did Jesus pray for the unity of believers? (17:21–22) (Believers, Jesus, Prayer)

When believers are unified, it helps to convince unbelievers of the truth of the gospel, and it reflects the unity of God the Father, Son, and Holy Spirit.

814. What did Jewish law require for sentencing? (18:13) (Jewish Practices)

In Jewish law, a person could not be sentenced on the same day his trial was held. The two examinations — this one and the one before Caiaphas — may have been conducted to create a sense of legitimacy.

815. Why would Jesus carry his own cross? (19:17) (Jesus, Punishment, Roman Practices)

To further humiliate him, the condemned person would normally carry a beam of the cross to the place of execution.

816. Why would a notice be attached to the cross? (19:19) (Roman Practices)

Often a placard would be attached to a cross stating the crime the person was being executed for. In this case, it stated that Jesus was the king of the Jews.

817. What was wine vinegar? (19:29) (Food)

This may have been cheap wine, the drink of ordinary people.

818. Why would the soldiers break the legs of those who were being crucified? (19:31) (Roman Practices)

This would make death come faster because the victim could not push himself up with his legs in order to get a full breath.

819. Who exactly was Joseph of Arimathea? (19:38) (Bible People)

Joseph of Arimathea was a rich member of the Sanhedrin and a secret follower of Jesus. He acted secretly because he was afraid of what the other Jewish leaders might do to him if they knew of his belief.

820. Can a person have doubts and still be a Christian? (20) (Christians, Doubts)

Having doubts about faith is not the same as saying that our faith isn't true. But when we wonder about the reality of God, we should pray, read the Bible, and talk to other believers. The Holy Spirit can use these things to help strengthen our faith.

Acts

821. Where did the ascension take place? (1:12) (Biblical Places)

☐▸ The ascension took place on the eastern slope of the Mount of Olives between Jerusalem and Bethany.

822. Why is Pentecost important in the history of the church? (2) (Church, Holy Spirit)

☐▸ Pentecost is said to be the beginning of the church. This was the time when God sent his Holy Spirit to the apostles so that they would begin preaching the Good News of Jesus to people from all different backgrounds.

823. What is the meaning of *baptism?*

(2) (Baptism, Meanings)

⬭➤ *Baptism* is a sign of the washing away of sin. Just as water washes dirt from a person's body, baptism is a sign that a person's sins are washed away, has been saved by grace, and belongs to God's family.

824. Is repentance necessary? (3:19)

(Repentance)

⬭➤ Yes. Repentance is a change of will and mind that arises from sorrow for sin and leads to a changed life.

825. What did the term *church* refer to?

(5:11) (Church, Meanings)

⬭➤ It could refer to the local congregation or to the universal church.

826. How did persecution help spread the gospel? (8:1) (Persecution)

☞ Because persecution broke out in Jerusalem, many of the believers scattered throughout Judea and Samaria, preaching the gospel wherever they went.

827. What was a centurion? (10:1) (Meanings, Roman Practices)

☞ A *centurion* was a Roman soldier who commanded a military unit of at least 100 other soldiers.

828. Who were God-fearers? (10:2) (Names)

☞ They were non-Jews who believed in God, attended the synagogue, and respected but did not practice all Jewish teachings.

829. Where did the term *Christian* come from? (11:26) (Christians, Meanings)

It isn't clear whether the term was first used by believers or was used in a negative way by nonbelievers. Literally, the word means "little messiahs" or "belonging to Christ."

830. Why was Saul's name changed by God? (13:9) (God's Love, Names)

Jews at this time often had two names: a Hebrew name (Saul) and a Greek-Roman name (Paul). Paul began to refer to himself as Paul from this point on, perhaps because of his mission to reach Gentiles.

831. What is *justification*? (13:39) (Meanings)

A person who believes in Jesus and asks for forgiveness is justified, or declared sinless, through Christ's death on the cross for our sins.

832. What must a person do to be saved? (16) (Salvation)

The only requirement for salvation is faith in Jesus. The Holy Spirit works in a person's heart before a person is able to believe in Jesus, but a person must also accept the grace that God has given.

833. How was Felix acquainted with the Way? (24:22) (Christians, Leaders)

He could not have governed Judea and Samaria for six years without becoming familiar with the activities of the Christians.

834. Why did Paul appeal to Caesar? (25:11) (Roman Practices)

Every Roman citizen had the right to have his case heard before Caesar or his representative. Winning such a case could have resulted in official recognition of Christianity as a religion separate from Judaism.

835. Why could Paul live by himself if he was in prison? (28:16) (Roman Practices)

☞ Paul had not committed any serious crime and was not politically dangerous, so he could live by himself with a guard assigned to him.

836. What was Paul's key message? (28:28) (Salvation)

☞ God's salvation had been sent to the Gentiles.

Romans

837. Why did Paul call himself a servant? (1:1) (Slaves)

☞ The Greek word Paul used literally meant "slave," but it could also mean a servant who willingly serves his master.

838. Did Paul think that anyone could be saved? (1:16–17) (Salvation)

▭► Yes, everyone who believes can be saved.

839. What is God's wrath like? (1:18) (Anger, God's Power)

▭► God's wrath is not impulsive anger. When people refuse to honor and obey him after God has revealed himself to them, he abandons them to their wickedness.

840. What did Paul mean by being judged apart from the law or under the law? (2:12–15) (Judgment, The Law)

▭► The Gentiles would be judged by how well they obeyed the laws written on their heart. The Jews, however, would be judged by how well they kept the law of Moses.

841. If we are saved by grace rather than works, is it okay to sin? (3:7–8)

(Grace, Sin)

☞ No. New life in Christ means putting aside our old, evil ways.

842. Why can no one be declared righteous by keeping the law? (3:20)

(Commandments, Perfection)

☞ No one can keep the law perfectly.

843. Why does the law bring wrath?

(4:15) (Anger, The Law)

☞ The law reveals sin, and since no one can keep the law perfectly, anyone who tries to earn salvation by keeping the law will face God's anger.

844. How did Paul define *hope*? (5:5) (Hope)

☞ Christian hope is based on God's love, revealed by the Holy Spirit, and demonstrated by the death of Christ.

845. If God forgives my sins, can I do whatever I want? (6) (Forgiveness, Sins)

The Bible is very clear that no one can keep God's law perfectly. But we still need to continue to strive to rid our lives of sin in thankfulness and service to God.

846. What is the significance of baptism? (6:3–4) (Baptism)

Through baptism, we are united with Christ, and we share in his death and resurrection so that we can have new life.

847. Was the law responsible for causing evil? (7:12–13) (The Law, Sin)

The law is holy and shines a light on sin and allows us to realize that because we are sinful we have to face the consequences.

848. How powerful is sin? (7:14–25) (Sin)

☞ Sin can take over, making people do what they don't want to do and keeping them from doing what they should do.

849. What are some of the ways that the Holy Spirit helps believers? (8)
(Believers, Holy Spirit)

☞ Those who belong to Christ have the Holy Spirit living in them. Their spirits are alive because of the work of the Holy Spirit, and the Holy Spirit also guarantees that they will live forever with Jesus. The Holy Spirit also helps Christians in their times of weakness and offers prayers that God will strengthen and help them.

850. What does it mean to be children of God? (8:14–17) (Family, Meanings)

☞ This refers to adoption. Adoption was common in Paul's time among the Greeks and Romans. An adopted child was granted all the privileges of a biological child, including the rights of inheritance. Christians are adopted by God through grace.

851. What hope do Christians have for the future? (8:23–25) (Christians, Hope)

⬚➤ Christians have already been adopted as God's children but look forward to eternal life and the resurrection of their bodies when Christ returns.

852. What pattern does God follow when he works in the hearts of his people? (8:30) (Salvation)

⬚➤ God chooses his people, calls them to himself, offers salvation through Christ, and promises them a glorious eternity.

853. Do Christians need to be afraid that God will stop loving them? (8:37–39)

(Christians, God's Love)

☞ Paul says that there is absolutely nothing that can separate a Christian from God's love.

854. When God chooses people for himself, is he being unfair to those he does not choose? (9:14–18)

(God's Power)

☞ Paul said that God has the sovereign right to grant mercy to whomever he chooses.

855. Why did Paul emphasize the importance of mission work?

(10:14–15) (God's Word)

☞ In order for people to hear the message and believe, others have to go out and tell them the Good News.

856. What was the remnant? (11:5) (Meanings)

There was a difference between God's covenant with the entire nation of Israel and with those who truly followed him. Although many Israelites rebelled against God, some remained faithful. These were the ones God had chosen by grace.

857. Does God care about sports? (12:5–8) (God's Love, Sports)

All of our gifts come from God. Some people are gifted with athletic ability, and God loves to see his children succeed but he also wants us to use his gifts to glorify him.

858. What does it mean to "bless those who persecute you"? (12:14) (Blessings, Persecution)

One of the basic principles Jesus taught his disciples was to treat others the way you want to be treated. This means being nice to people even when they've been unkind to you.

859. Does God want us to follow unfair rules? (13:1–3) (Fairness, Leaders)

Even if it isn't fair, God wants us to follow people who have authority over us because it honors him.

860. Why are Christians expected to obey the government authorities? (13:1–5) (Leaders, Obedience)

A practical reason is to avoid punishment. But the more important reason is that governments are given authority by God to maintain order in society and to administer justice.

861. What did Paul urge believers who had different practices or opinions to do? (14:4, 10–12) (Judgment)

He told them not to judge each other for these differences because each Christian answers to God for his behavior. Christians are not to put themselves in God's place as judge.

862. What sort of peace should Christians promote among themselves? (14:19-21) (Christians, Peace)

Christians should work for peaceful relationships and to build one another up.

863. How does Scripture help Christians? (15:4) (Christians, God's Word)

Paul said that Scripture was written for our instruction so that as we patiently endure we will be encouraged to hold fast to our hope in Christ.

1 Corinthians

864. What does it mean to be sexually pure? (6) (Sex)

God created human beings as sexual creatures, and sex is a good gift from God that brings pleasure to people, unites them in a relationship, and is necessary for having children. But God wants people to use this gift in the right way. That means that only people who are married should have sex. The Holy Spirit lives inside each of us, and we should honor and respect our bodies and not use our bodies in ways that would dishonor God.

865. What did Paul mean when he said, "each person should remain in the situation he or she was in when God called them"? (7:20–23) (Meanings)

Paul said each person should be content to live for the Lord in whatever economic or social situation he or she was in when they became a Christian. The important thing was to have a godly attitude.

866. How are Christians supposed to honor the consciences of fellow believers? (8) (Christians, Honor)

☞ Christians should be sensitive to the consciences of other Christians and not do anything that would lead others to sin or give unbelievers a reason to criticize them or their faith.

867. What are spiritual gifts? (12) (Blessings, Holy Spirit)

☞ God has given his people gifts through the Holy Spirit. The Bible says that there are a variety of gifts that God gives. These gifts may include the ability to teach, to preach, to prophesy, to heal, to give leadership, to help people in need, to serve others, to encourage others, to show love, and many others. We discover our gifts by looking at what we do well when we are working with other Christians. Once we discover our gifts, it is important for us to use them to serve God and other people — both within the church and in the larger community in which we live.

868. What is "speaking in different kinds of tongues"? (12:10) (Language, Meanings)

👉 Some people think this refers to a person's ability to speak in a human language that he or she has never learned, which is what the apostles did on Pentecost. Others think it refers to speaking in a heavenly type of language of praise and prayer when a person is overcome by the Holy Spirit.

869. What is the most important message of the gospel? (15:3–4) (Jesus, Salvation)

👉 The core message of the gospel is that Jesus died for our sins, that he was buried, and that he rose from the dead.

870. What is the victory God gives to Christians? (15:57) (Salvation)

👉 Sin brought death into the world, and people were judged under the law, which showed us our sin. But Christ paid the price for our sin by dying and rising again. Thus sin and death no longer have power over a believer.

2 Corinthians

871. When should people in the church forgive someone who has sinned?

(2:5–11) (Church, Forgiveness, Sin)

▭➔ A member of the church in Corinth had committed a serious sin, and the church had disciplined him. Now Paul said that he should be forgiven and taken back into the church because he was truly sorry for his sin.

872. What have people who have been forgiven called to do? (5:18–20)

(Forgiveness)

▭➔ People who have been restored to a right relationship with God through believing in Jesus as their Savior are called to tell the world about God's love.

873. Why can't I wait to become a Christian until after I've had my fun? (6) (Forgiveness, Sin)

When God calls us, we should not resist the Holy Spirit working in our heart. If we do not respond to his call, we are insulting God and acting as if his gift of salvation is not important. By becoming a Christian when God calls us, we can benefit from participating with other believers as we grow in our faith and do God's work in the world which is the most fun life of all!

874. What does the Bible teach about giving money? (8–9) (Money)

God told people to take special care of those who could not take care of themselves, such as widows and orphans. Christians should give generously to the church and other good causes because everything that they have is a gift from God, and they should be eager to use their resources to support God's work. Our gifts will help other people, will reflect our gratitude to God, and will cause others who see our generosity to praise God.

Galatians

875. Does God love people of different backgrounds, races, and cultures?
(3) (God's Love)

▭⟶ Yes. God's message is one of diversity and inclusiveness. Before Jesus ascended to heaven, he told his followers to go throughout the world, making disciples of all nations.

876. How are believers "children of God"? (3:26–29) (Believers, Family)

▭⟶ All who believe in Christ are called children of God.

877. How can Christians overcome sinful desires? (5:16) (Sin)

▭⟶ Living by the promptings and power of the Spirit can keep us from giving in to temptation.

Ephesians

878. Do we choose God, or did God choose us? (1:4–5, 11) (God's Power)

In his letters, Paul emphasized the fact that God chose his people.

879. Why are some people saved and not others? (2) (Free Will, Salvation)

We are not responsible for our own salvation, but we can choose to accept God's gift or refuse it.

880. What is the role of leaders in the church? (4:11–12) (Church, Leaders)

Leaders are not supposed to do all the work themselves but are supposed to train others and prepare them for works of service.

881. What is the new self? (4:24) (Believers)

When someone becomes a believer, through Christ he becomes a new person.

882. Do I always need to obey my parents? (6:1–3) (Obedience, Parents)

God gave you your parents to protect and help you; and in order for them to do that, you have to obey them.

Philippians

883. What did it mean to "work out your salvation with fear and trembling"?
(2:12) (Fear, Salvation)

Paul didn't mean that Christians had to earn their salvation, which is impossible. He meant that they should seek spiritual growth and development because of their reverence and awe for God.

884. What is the peace of God? (4:7) (Peace)

This is not just a feeling of relaxation but a deep inner contentment that comes from the knowledge that you are at peace with God because he has forgiven your sins.

Colossians

885. Why do we have to go to church?
(1) (Church)

In a church, Christians can hear ministers and teachers explain God's Word and what it means for people's lives. If we simply read the Bible on our own, we may not understand parts of it or we may form wrong ideas. Church is also a place where people can gather to give praise and honor to God as a group. We go to church to encourage one another and build each other up in our faith. Fellow Christians can help to strengthen our faith, correct us when we make mistakes, support us when we face difficult times, and share our joys and sorrows. Finally, we can serve God more effectively through evangelism and service projects by joining with other Christians than we could on our own.

886. What are the three great Christian virtues? (1:5) (Faith, Hope, Love)

They are faith, hope, and love.

887. What was the mystery of God?
(1:25–26) (Faith, Grace, Meanings)

Paul used the word to refer to God's plans that were revealed through Christ: Salvation comes to all who by grace through faith believe in him.

1 Thessalonians

888. What does the Bible teach about the return of Jesus? (4–5) (Jesus)

Whether Jesus returns during our lifetimes or later is not important. We should not live in fear, but we should have confidence that we will live with Jesus forever because he has paid the price for sin, and we should encourage fellow Christians with this truth.

2 Thessalonians

889. Will people who have never heard of God be punished when Jesus returns? (1:8) (Punishment, Unbelievers)

▢➤ In this verse, Paul was writing about punishment for those who had heard but still refused to believe in and follow God and accept the gospel of Jesus.

890. What are God's teachings about work? (3) (Hard Work)

▢➤ The Bible tells us that work is important and that we should not be lazy. Christians should use the talents that God has given them and should see their jobs as a way of serving God and other people.

1 Timothy

891. How was Christ a ransom? (2:6)
(Meanings)

> The Greek word for *ransom* usually referred to the price paid to free a slave. Jesus gave his life to free people from their sins.

892. Why is it important for girls to dress modestly? (2:9–10) (Clothing, Women)

> The body is the temple of the Holy Spirit. Dressing modestly shows respect for God and the body God has given each of us.

893. Does God think that women are less important than men? (2:11–15) (Women)

> God loves both men and women equally. These guidelines were just expressing an opinion that was appropriate for the culture Paul lived in.

894. Is it wrong for women to teach or preach? (2:12–14) (Women)

Some think Paul was prohibiting women from teaching or exercising authority over men in all times and places. Others think he meant that women who had not been properly taught (like the women of Ephesus) should not attempt to teach. Still others think Paul was expressing an opinion that was appropriate for the culture in which he lived but that does not apply to today's world.

895. What is the responsibility of the church for people who have special needs? (5) (Church, The Poor)

The emphasis throughout the Bible is that God's people should care for one another. God has given his love generously to his people, and in a spirit of thankfulness and love, believers should give generously — time, money, or help — to others.

896. Did Paul think that Christians should live in poverty? (6:6–10)

(Material Possessions)

Paul said that being godly was better than being rich, and he also pointed out that the desire to become rich led some to wander from their faith and do evil deeds.

897. Is it wrong to want to be rich?

(6:9–11) (Material Possessions, Money)

Everyone wants to have enough money for the things they need. But God doesn't want his followers to become so caught up in making money it is all they think about.

898. What were the wealthy Christians supposed to do with their money?

(6:17–19) (Money)

Paul said that they should put their hope in God rather than in their riches. He also said they should be generous and share their wealth with others.

2 Timothy

899. Is the Bible really God's Word?

(3) (The Bible, God's Word)

▭⟶ Yes. The books of the Bible were written by many authors over several centuries, but the message of the Bible is unified. People believe that the Bible is truly God's Word because the Holy Spirit creates faith in their hearts, allowing them to see what God has done and plans to do for his people.

900. Why is knowledge of Scripture so important? (3:14–17) (God's Word)

▭⟶ Paul said that Scripture is inspired by God and contains the truths people need to know in order to gain faith in Jesus. Scripture is also useful for teaching people how to live in a way that pleases God.

Titus

901. What effect did grace have on believers? (2:11–14) (Grace, Salvation)

God's grace brought salvation, and it also helped people reject worldliness and live godly lives.

902. How were the Christians to deal with troublemakers and false teachers? (3:10) (Unbelievers)

After warning a person twice, they were to have nothing to do with the person. The people who were spreading false doctrines were excommunicated from the church in the hope that they might repent and in order to protect those in the church from falsehood.

Philemon/Hebrews

903. How did the author prove that Jesus was superior to the angels?

(1:5–14) (Angels, Jesus)

☞ He proved this by quoting seven passages from the Old Testament to show that Jesus is God's Son, that angels worship him, and that he is God.

904. What relationship do believers have with God? (2:10–11) (Believers, Family, God)

☞ Believers become children of God because of the sacrifice of Jesus. And Jesus becomes a brother to Christians.

905. How are believers like God's house?

(3:6) (Believers, Symbols)

☞ God lives with them, and they are members of his family and household.

906. What is the importance of holding firmly to the faith? (3:14) (Faith)

Continuing in faith rather than falling away shows that a person is truly a Christian.

907. Does God know everything that I do or think? (4) (God's Power)

One of God's characteristics is that he is omniscient (all-knowing). God knows everything perfectly about the past, present, and future. God loves us in spite of the things that we do that disappoint him. The fact that God knows everything can be a source of comfort for Christians because even though God can see our sins, he also sees the faith that we have in our hearts, and he knows us as his children.

908. How do believers enter God's rest?

(4:3) (Believers, Peace)

Believers enter God's rest today when they have faith in Jesus. As a result, Christians have rest now and in the future because of the peace of knowing that God is with them and that they will spend eternity with Jesus.

909. How was Jesus like and unlike other human beings? (4:15) (Jesus, Perfection, Sin)

Jesus was like other human beings because he faced every kind of temptation a person can have. But unlike any other person, he did not sin.

910. How was Jesus made "perfect"?

(5:8–10) (Jesus, Perfection, Suffering)

Jesus perfectly fulfilled his purpose here on earth through suffering and dying on the cross for our sins.

911. How can we draw near to God?

(10:22) (God's Presence)

☐ First, a person should have a sincere heart devoted only to God. Second, a person should have full assurance of faith and no second thoughts about trusting Jesus. Third, a person should have a conscience free from guilt because of Christ's sacrifice. Fourth, a person's heart should be washed of sin as symbolized by baptism.

912. What is *faith*? (11) (Faith, Meanings)

☐ *Faith* is the response of a believer to God's revelation of himself. A person who has faith believes that everything that the Bible teaches about God is completely true and trustworthy. Faith is not something that we create for ourselves; it is a gift of the Holy Spirit who works in our hearts.

James

913. Are people saved by faith alone or by faith and good deeds? (2) (Faith)

What James is saying is that if a person has faith, then he or she will demonstrate that faith by living a life that is pleasing to God.

914. Can faith and good deeds exist independently? (2:17–18) (Faith)

James said that faith and deeds must accompany each other. Faith without actions is dead. When we have faith, we are eager to do good deeds.

915. Are some people judged more strictly than others? (3:1) (Judgment, Leaders)

James said that people like teachers or ministers who have greater responsibility and influence will be judged according to how they use that power.

916. Why does James speak so strongly against friendship with the world?

(4:4) (Friendship)

He is referring to an attitude of rebellion against God and his laws. James said that becoming friendly with the sinful world is like committing adultery toward God.

917. What is *slander*? (4:11–12) (Meanings)

Slander is saying false things about another person. More broadly, it is speaking critically or negatively about someone behind their back.

918. Is it wrong to make plans? (4:13–15) (God's Power)

Planning ahead is something the Bible encourages. But we need to realize that God is in charge, and our plans should reflect the godly way he wants us to live.

919. Will prayer always lead to healing?

(5:15–16) (Prayer, Sickness)

It is important to ask God for healing, but many Christians continue to have health problems and Christians continue to die. Even if God doesn't heal our bodies, he will always forgive our sins if we ask in faith.

1 Peter

920. What does it mean to be "redeemed"? (1:18) (Meanings)

Redeem means to free from captivity.

921. Why are Christians supposed to obey rulers and other authorities?

(2:13–15) (Leaders, Obedience)

God is the one who allows human authority and governments to exist, so obeying rulers — as long as it doesn't conflict with God's laws — is like obeying God.

922. Is it wrong for girls to get dressed up? (3:2–5) (Clothing, Women)

No. God is just saying that inner beauty and serving him is more beautiful than wearing fancy clothes.

923. How should Christians behave if they are not treated fairly? (3:9)
(Fairness, Hardship)

Peter said that believers should not seek revenge but should show kindness even to those who treat them poorly.

924. What is *baptism*? (3:21) (Baptism, Meanings)

Baptism is a personal commitment to Jesus and a symbol for the washing away of sin but also the promise of salvation through Christ.

925. How are Christians supposed to resist the devil? (5:8–9) (Faith, Satan)

Christians resist the devil by being self-controlled and alert to his ways and by standing firm in their faith. Christians should pray for each other for strength to withstand temptation.

2 Peter

926. How does God deal with wicked people such as false teachers? (2:9) (Judgment, Repentance)

Wicked people face the consequences of their actions; and if they die unrepentant, they will face judgment.

927. What did Peter say about God's view of time? (3:8–9) (God's Power, Humans, Time)

Peter said that God was not bound by the human understanding of time.

1 John

928. Are Christians required to obey God's laws? (2:4–5) (The Law, Perfection)

No one can keep God's laws perfectly, but Christians obey God's laws as a way of expressing thankfulness for his gift of salvation.

929. Who is the antichrist? (2:18) (Meanings, Satan)

John's definition of an antichrist is probably anyone who opposes Jesus Christ.

930. Are Christians perfect? (3:9–10) (Christians, Perfection)

No. Even Christians sin, but overall their lives should not be characterized by sin but by doing what God requires.

931. Is it possible to be saved by believing in the Father but not the Son? (3:23) (Salvation, Trinity)

No, if we deny the Son, we do not have the Father. If we believe in Jesus, we believe also in God.

932. How can Christians be confident of their salvation? (4:17) (Christians, Salvation)

If Christians (people who acknowledge that Jesus is the Son of God) are like Christ in their love, this is a sign that God lives in them and has given the gift of salvation.

933. What sin leads to death? (5:16) (Death, Sin)

Denying the truth about Jesus or continuing to commit sins without repenting can lead to separation from God and spiritual death.

934. Why doesn't God always answer our prayers? (1 John 5) (Prayer)

God has a plan for each person, and he knows what is best for each of us. We may pray for God to do certain things, but we must also be willing to accept the fact that God's will may not be the same as ours. Regardless, we can be sure that God loves us and cares for us.

2 John

935. What was the Bible written on? (1:12) (The Bible)

The paper was made from papyrus reeds and the ink was made by mixing carbon, water, and gum or oil.

3 John

936. What was a sign that a person was a Christian? (v. 11) (Christians)

John said that if a person continually did good works, the person was from God. On the other hand, if a person continually did evil, that person was not from God.

Jude

937. How does it make God feel when we sin even though we know it's wrong? (1:4) (Sin)

The Bible says that this perverts the grace of God and takes advantage of his forgiveness. People who truly want to follow God will try their hardest to always follow God.

Revelation

938. Why did God say he was the Alpha and the Omega? (1:8) (God's Power, Symbols)

These are the first and last letters in the Greek alphabet. God is the beginning and the end.

939. What is the Lord's Day? (1:10) (Sabbath, Meanings)

Sunday was called the Lord's Day because that was the day Jesus rose from the dead.

940. What is the book of life? (3:5) (Meanings)

The book of life is a record of all the names of those who believe in Jesus as their Lord and Savior and will live forever with God.

941. What is the Abyss? (9:1) (Hell, Meanings)

This is thought to be the bottomless underground pit where demons live.

942. What was the mystery of God?
(10:7) (God's Power)

▢⟶ The mystery was that God had won the victory over the forces of evil and would reign forever.

943. Who was Michael? (12:7) (Angels)

▢⟶ Michael was the archangel who defeated Satan in heavenly warfare. As a result, Satan was hurled out of heaven onto the earth.

944. Can the devil read our minds? (12:9)
(Satan)

▢⟶ The devil leads us astray by understanding how we think and deceiving and tempting us but he does not know our thoughts.

945. What will heaven look like? (21–22)
(Heaven)

▢⟶ John wrote about his vision of heaven describing it as a place of great beauty and light. He compared it to a city that had streets of gold and walls covered with precious stones. But heaven is far beyond human comprehension; all we know is that it will be more beautiful than anything we can imagine.

946. What will heaven be like? (21–22)
(Heaven)

Heaven is where God's people will live with him forever, far beyond our ability to describe in human terms. Heaven is a place where there will be no sin or sadness. It will be a place of perfection, where we will live with God and see him face to face for all of eternity.

947. What will the new heaven and earth be like? (21:2–22:5) (Heaven)

It will be a place of perfection where people will live with God and where there will be no sorrow or death.

Miscellaneous

948. Why do we study the Bible?
(The Bible, Faith, God's Word)

The Bible is God's Word. Without it, we are truly lost. But by reading and studying the Bible, we learn about God and can learn how to live the way God wants us to live. Reading and studying the Bible makes it possible for us to get closer to God, and become more like him every day.

949. What language was the Bible originally written in? (The Bible, Language)

The Old Testament was written in Hebrew and some Aramaic; the New Testament was written in Greek.

950. Who wrote the Bible? (The Bible, God's Word)

The Bible was written under the inspiration of God by over 40 different authors from all walks of life: shepherds, farmers, tent-makers, physicians, fishermen, priests, philosophers, and kings.

951. Who was the first human to be inspired to write the Bible, and when did he start? (The Bible, Bible People)

Moses began writing about the year 1500 BC.

952. Who wrote the last book of the Bible and when? (The Bible, Time)

John wrote the book of Revelation about AD 90.

953. What single author contributed the most to the Old Testament? (The Bible, Bible People)

Moses contributed the most to the Old Testament. He wrote the first five books of the Bible.

954. What single author contributed the most to the New Testament? (The Bible, Bible People)

The apostle Paul wrote 14 books of the New Testament, over half of that part of the Bible.

955. Where did the Bible get its name?
(The Bible, Meanings)

The Bible gets its name from a Greek word that means "the little book." Gradually the word began to mean "holy book."

956. What is the name for the first five books of the Bible? (The Bible, Meanings)

The first five books are called the *Pentateuch*. The names of the books are: Genesis, Exodus, Leviticus, Numbers, and Deuteronomy.

957. When was the Bible first translated into English? (The Bible, Time)

The Bible was translated into English in 1382, by John Wycliffe.

958. When was the Bible first printed on a printing press? (The Bible, Time)

The Bible was first printed on a press in 1454 by Johannes Gutenberg. It was the first book ever printed.

959. How many languages has the Bible been translated into? (The Bible, Languages)

The Bible has been translated into approximately 2,000 languages with a countless number of partial as well as audio translations.

960. Are there errors in the Bible? (The Bible)

Some people say there are contradictions in the Bible, but because of the difficulty in translating the Bible it's most likely that communicating the original message is difficult because of the limitations of its original language.

961. What are the two main parts of the Bible? (The Bible)

The Bible is divided into two main parts. The Old Testament tells about God's love story with the world, from his creation of everything up to the time of Jesus. The New Testament tells us about Jesus and his mission here on earth, as well as the mission of the disciples after him, spreading the Word of God.

962. What does the word *testament* mean? (The Bible, Meanings)

The word *testament* means "covenant" or "contract."

963. How many books are in the NIV Bible? (The Bible)

There are a total of 66 books in the NIV Bible — 39 Old Testament and 27 New Testament.

964. Why are there different versions of the Bible? (The Bible)

The Bible had to be translated because it was originally written in Hebrew, Aramaic, and Greek. There are many ways to translate the original version of the Bible, so there are many different versions that focus on different things or are written in different ways.

965. What is a *parable*? (Parables)

A *parable* is a made-up story that helps us understand something. Jesus told many parables to get his points across. The people in the parables did not actually exist, but the stories can help us to understand important truths. Examples are found in: Luke 15:11–32; Mark 4:1–20.

966. What are *angels*? (Angels)

The word *angel* is a Greek word that means "messenger"—so angels are God's messengers. Even though we can't see them, angels play a big part in life as noted in the Bible, where angels are mentioned over 200 times. Angels can be both good and bad and there are different types of angels such as archangels, cherubim, and seraphim. Michael, Gabriel, and Lucifer are probably three of the most well-known angels from the Bible.

967. What is the last word in the Bible?
(The Bible)

☞ *Amen*. It is in Revelation 22:21.

968. What is the longest word in the Bible? (The Bible)

☞ *Maher-Shalal-Hash-Baz*, found in Isaiah 8:1.

969. What is the longest book in the Bible? (The Bible)

☞ The book of Psalms is the longest. It has 150 chapters.

970. What is the shortest book in the Bible? (The Bible)

☞ The Third Book of John is the shortest book.

971. How many times does the word God appear in the Bible? (The Bible)

☞ The word *God* appears 3,358 times in the Bible, in every book except Esther and the Song of Songs.

972. What is taught about anger in the Bible? (Anger, The Bible)

☞ Sometimes anger is justified, such as when God is angered by human sin (Numbers 32:13) but when anger is unjustified it is a sin (Luke 15:28). Anger must be controlled and properly directed.

973. Who was the oldest person in the Bible? (Age, The Bible, Bible People)

☞ Methuselah, mentioned in Genesis 5:27, was the oldest person mentioned in the Bible. His age at death was 969 years old.

974. How many verses are in the Bible?
(The Bible)

▭▶ There are 31,173 verses in the Bible: 23,214 in the Old Testament and 7,959 in the New. Each gospel of the Bible was written for a specific reason and group of people.

975. For whom was the book of Matthew written? (The Bible)

▭▶ Matthew was written for the Jewish people.

976. Who exactly was Matthew? (The Bible, Bible People)

▭▶ Matthew was a "publican" who became one of the twelve apostles. A publican was a tax collector.

977. For whom was the book of Mark written? (The Bible)

▭▶ Mark was written for the Gentiles — those people who were not Jewish.

978. Who exactly was Mark? (The Bible, Bible People)

Mark was a strong believer in Jesus during his life and then became a prominent church leader after Jesus' death.

979. For whom was the book of Luke written? (The Bible)

Luke was written for any person who wanted to know the kind of person Jesus was.

980. Who exactly was Luke? (The Bible, Bible People)

Luke was a Greek physician who was born in Syria. He was a good friend of the apostle Paul.

981. For whom was the book of John written? (The Bible)

John was written for everyone who wants to understand who Jesus really is.

982. Who exactly was John? (The Bible, Bible People)

▢☞ John was one of Jesus' closest disciples. He was "the disciple that Jesus loved."

983. Why is the Bible divided into verses and chapters? (The Bible)

▢☞ In the original text of the various books of the Bible, there are no such things as chapter and verse divisions. They were added later for the sake of convenience.

984. What is the shortest verse in the Bible? (The Bible)

▢☞ John 11:35 — "Jesus wept" — is the shortest verse in most English versions of the Bible.

985. How many books of the Bible were written by women? (The Bible, Women)

While some of the books in the Bible are about women, it is widely believed that there were no female authors of the Bible.

986. What is the longest chapter in the Bible? (The Bible, Psalms)

The longest chapter of the Bible is Psalm 119.

987. What is the longest psalm? (The Bible, Psalms)

Psalm 119 is the longest psalm in the Bible.

988. What is the shortest chapter in the Bible? (The Bible)

The shortest chapter in the Bible is Psalm 117.

989. The ark was measured in cubits. How long is a cubit? (Ancient Practices)

The cubit was a common form of measurement in the Old Testament. The length of a cubit was usually based on the distance between the elbow and the fingertip, so the cubit varied in length but probably averaged about 19.8 inches.

990. Where is Mount Sinai? (Biblical Places)

Mount Sinai is arguably one of the most famous biblical locations. It was where Moses received the Ten Commandments from God. It is said to be located on the Sinai Peninsula in Egypt.

991. Were the Judges in the Bible really judges? (Ancient Practices)

There were twelve main Judges in the Old Testament: Othniel, Ehud, Shamgar, Deborah, Gideon, Tola, Jair, Jephthah, Ibzan, Elon, Abdon, and Samson. They acted mainly as military leaders but also presided over legal hearings.

992. Was Goliath really a giant man?
(Bible People)

The oldest manuscripts of the Bible, the Dead Sea Scrolls, give Goliath's height as "four cubits and a span," which would be about six feet seven. Later manuscripts increase his height to "six cubits and a span" making him nine feet tall.

993. Do we know for sure that Christmas/Jesus' birth was December 25? (Bible People, Jesus)

The Bible does not mention an exact date that Jesus was born. By the late fourth century, it was generally celebrated in churches on December 25. This date provided a Christian alternative to pagan festivals related to the Roman god Saturn and the winter solstice.

994. What language did Jesus speak as he preached to the people? (Jesus, Language)

He most likely spoke Aramaic.

995. Why do many Bible people have such unusual names? (Ancient Practices, Bible People)

People in Bible times named their children common names in their language. Our names would sound unusual to them if they heard ours. One thing to remember is that Jewish people took great care in naming their children, making sure of the meaning of the name and how it would affect their lives.

996. Why does the Bible refer to God in masculine terms? (The Bible)

This is the way God has chosen to reveal himself to us. God is never described with sexual characteristics in the Scriptures, but he does consistently describe himself in the masculine gender including words like: King, Father, Judge, Husband, Master, and the God and Father of our Lord Jesus Christ. This is even reflected in the Incarnation.

997. How much of the Bible is a myth and how much is real? (The Bible)

▭➤ Amazing things happen in the Bible, like the story of Jonah being swallowed by a huge fish. And no matter how unbelievable some of the stories seem, everything is possible when God is part of the story, as God is in the entire Bible. The Bible's miracles were a demonstration of God's power and authority.

998. Does the Bible tell us everything we need to know about God?

(The Bible, God's Word)

▭➤ For almost 2,000 years Christians have agreed that the Bible alone is God's Word, and that it tells us everything we need to know about him.

999. Is God a God of love? Some of the stories in the Old Testament seem to contradict that. (God's Love)

It is important to remember that, while God is a God of love, he is also a holy God, separate from sinners and perfect in righteousness, justice, and purity. Judgment against rebellious and indifferent sinners is inevitable, apart from repentance, "for the wages of sin is death" (Romans 6:23a).

1000. In the Bible is there any description of Jesus as a child? (The Bible, Jesus)

We read that Jesus grew in wisdom and stature. He was human, after all, and so naturally he grew physically, mentally, and spiritually. One important thing to remember is found in Hebrews 4:15, Jesus was "tempted in every way, just as we are — yet he did not sin."

1001. Do many people read the Bible? (The Bible)

Yes. The Bible has sold the most copies of any book ever published.

Index of Topics

352 1001 Bible Questions Kids Ask